ALL ABOUT THE MONEY, HONEY!

Recipes for Financial Success

ALL ABOUT THE MONEY, HONEY!

Recipes for Financial Success

JULIANNE DOWLING

Wrightbooks

First published 2008 by Wrightbooks
an imprint of John Wiley & Sons Australia, Ltd
42 McDougall Street, Milton Qld 4064

Office also in Melbourne
Typeset in Adobe Caslon Pro 11.5/16 pt

© Julianne Dowling 2008
The moral rights of the author have been asserted.

National Library of Australia Cataloguing-in-Publication data:

Dowling, Julianne.
All about the money, honey : recipes for financial success.
Includes index.
ISBN 9780731406609 (pbk.).
1. Women — Australia — Finance, Personal.
2. Finance, Personal — Australia. I. Title.
332.0240082

All rights reserved. Except as permitted under the *Australian Copyright Act 1968* (for example, a fair dealing for the purposes of study, research, criticism or review), no part of this book may be reproduced, stored in a retrieval system, communicated or transmitted in any form or by any means without prior written permission. All inquiries should be made to the publisher at the address above.

The AMP.NATSEM Reports were written by the National Centre for Social and Economic Modelling Pty Limited ('NATSEM') and published by AMP.

CHOICE data reprinted from <www.choice.com.au> (Online 14/08/07) with the permission of CHOICE.

Cover design by popomo designs
Author image by Michael Kennedy Photography
Printed by McPherson's Printing Group
10 9 8 7 6 5 4 3 2 1

Disclaimer

The material in this publication is of the nature of general comment only, and neither purports nor intends to be advice. Readers should not act on the basis of any matter in this publication without considering (and if appropriate taking) professional advice with due regard to their own particular circumstances. The author and publisher expressly disclaim all and any liability to any person, whether a purchaser of this publication or not, in respect of anything and of the consequences of anything done or omitted to be done by any such person in reliance, whether in whole or in part, upon the whole or any part of the contents of this publication.

Foreword by Jean Kittson

When I was a 15-year-old girl, I took my first holiday job as a waitress in the local bistro—whatever happened to bistros?—and I earned my first money, and my mother gave me some invaluable financial advice. I'd saved $350 by the end of the summer holidays, and she drove me along a sandy road to a scrubby backblock with a 'For Sale' sign hammered onto a twisty tea-tree, where she said, 'Buy this land. It's for sale for $350'. So I did. Two years later I sold it for a 100 per cent profit. Yes, I sold it for $700, and I bought my first car. A Wolseley 24/80. Today the block of land is worth $600 000, and the car is worth about $50 in unpaid parking fines.

The moral is, young women, listen to your mother when she tells you to buy a block of land. Do not then listen to your father when he says: 'A block of land won't take you to the drive-in. Buy a car'.

Let this book be your mother. If I had read this book back then, I would now reign over a real estate empire. I would be the Donald Trump of Tootgarook. I would have collected land like Madonna collects Manolo Blahniks. I would have negative geared with such finesse that my dog would have been tax deductible. As it was, the only leveraging I ever did was when I promised to do housecleaning for the local mechanic if he fixed my Wolseley. He was my dad. The only negative gearing I experienced was when the clutch gave out.

It wasn't so long ago that the first financial advice given to most women was when their mothers made them tie their lunch money in the corner of their hankies so they didn't lose it, and they were told to give it to the teacher straightaway when they got to school. The next financial advice a woman was given was when the bank manager told her not to trouble her pretty head with sums, and could she ask her husband to give him a call.

This approach may have inspired generations of women to anger, silent bloodlust and possibly divorce, but it didn't inspire them to financial confidence.

Happily, inspiration and confidence is what *All About the Money, Honey* is all about. This wonderful guide to self-fulfilment in fiscal terms will explain where your money comes from (your efforts) and what it can do (generate more money) and who for (you). Because you deserve it. It is clear and wonderfully easy to understand, with a wealth of encouraging anecdotes and level, woman-to-woman advice. If you thought spending money was fun, just wait until you read this book and start making it—with your own fair hands, and your own pretty little head. Julianne Dowling makes you believe that you truly can control a portfolio of shares or an investment property or even a credit card in meltdown as easily as you can manage a family, a husband or your hair.

I want *All About the Money, Honey* to be a school text. I

want my daughters to read it immediately and start putting their pocket money to work, or even giving it back to me to make it work for them. I will also keep the books (heh, heh).

Julianne Dowling is the Jamie Oliver of finance, the Nigella Lawson, the fiscal Bocuse. This is not a random comparison. Along with real-life examples of inspiring, path-finding women, this book has actual, living recipes for financial success. The ingredients are already yours, awaiting only the sure touch Julianne Dowling brings, and which she is so generously eager to share.

Jean Kittson

Contents

Preface xi

About the author xiii

Acknowledgements xiv

1 Into the Kitchen 1
2 Cutting Back on Sweets 21
3 Out of the Frying Pan 39
4 Beyond Home Economics 57
5 Dinner for One 83
6 Chief Cook and Bottle-washer? 101
7 The Super Souffle 127
8 Investing: the Smorgasbord 157
9 The Catering Conundrum 183
10 Top Tips from Cluey Cooks 207

Index 231

Preface

So many money books are about the rational, and yet when it comes to making financial decisions, we know that life can sometimes sway us off what seems to be the right course of action!

This book seeks to combine the insights of experts with the real-life experiences (and ideas) of Aussie women. The 'deadly Ds'—death of a partner, divorce or separation and debt—may feel like the really big cannonballs in life, but curveballs can also be thrown at us in the form of dependants and limited cash flow. Money can wear us down because it governs so many choices—where we live, what our retirement prospects are and whether we can afford to have children.

To me, thinking about financial plans as financial recipes feels so right. So much of our lives is spent on domestic minutiae; why not look at our finances through a similar filter? Good food is about assembling the best ingredients, working on making the dish perfect and investing some 'heart' into the outcome. Good money management is a bit like that, too.

One thing I found during my research is that women really want to know what their peers are up to as a way of benchmarking their own lives and learning fresh strategies for their own situations.

I was surprised at how quickly women reached their goals when they had a financial plan! During the 'cooking' phase of this book, three women managed to save enough to buy property with partners and family, despite having limited funds earlier on. Other women dug their way out of deep debt or restarted their savings from scratch.

It's sad but true that women have a tendency to switch off instead of learning financial skills, and that some of us look for Mr Right or Mr Not-So-Right as a rescue remedy. But the stories here show that we're capable of much more than that! Of course, there isn't a magic bullet to getting ahead, but being independent both in spirit and finances is a wise goal.

Independence is also about financial up-skilling. Learning the 'recipes' and applying them to your financial situation can make a real difference! Being confident and listening to your values is also part of the financial fitness equation.

If this book is your first step into a new financial frontier, then take heart. Using the insights of other women—celebrities, financial experts and clinical psychologist Dorothea Vallianos—I hope you'll come to see through your own experience that not only is knowledge power, but that sometimes just changing your thinking about life (and money) makes a real difference.

Julianne Dowling
Sydney, NSW
October 2007

About the author

Julianne Dowling is a freelance financial journalist with a background in financial services. Her articles on money have appeared in *Notebook:* magazine, *Vive* magazine, *The Australian*, *Money Management*, *Australian Property Investor* and *CPA In the Black*. She's also an experienced investor who has built and sold a successful business.

Acknowledgements

Now that I've finished, I confess I'll rather miss not having a good reason to probe people about their lives and finances 'for the book'. I must have interviewed nearly 100 women and appreciate such a generous wellspring of stories, friendship, practical tips and ideas! I'd like to single out Clemence Harvey and Jac Phillips, ANZ Bank's National Marketing Manager—Financial Planning, for special praise. Clem pushed me to take my initial ideas beyond being just ideas. Jac kept me on track with encouragement, info from the bank and an introduction to Jean Kittson. They both injected laughs, a few prods and breezy enthusiasm when these were most needed. Big thanks also go to Dorothea Vallianos in Brisbane, who brought her expertise to the psychological side of money management and contributed much to the book generally. Again, many thanks to the 30 experts within the pages of the book, particularly those from ANZ, and to the team at Wiley who have made it all possible.

Chapter 1
Into the Kitchen

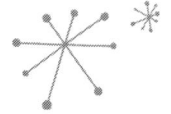

> *I'm in the process of finding my 'financial self' after having a good time.*
> —Jo Cowling, *The Biggest Loser* contestant and real-estate marketing manager

'I'm no good with money.' 'I don't have enough.' 'It's not important.' 'Maybe you should ask someone who knows!' Sound familiar? Many women—even wise and successful ones—respond like this when asked about the crunchy stuff.

Feminist Simone de Beauvoir nailed it when she said that we women need to get our financial affairs sorted to be truly independent. So why is it that so many of us are still playing catch-up when we enter our middle years?

It can be hard to apply advice and insights from those in the know to our own not-so-straightforward lives. Sometimes it's hard even to know where to start, and inertia can be the biggest enemy of all. Trouble is, money just doesn't feel so *easy*.

When I first sat down to write this book, my close friend Dorothea Vallianos, a Brisbane-based clinical psychologist, had some great insights to offer. Dorothea believes we should 'reframe' money, and compares it to cooking. 'Sometimes, if you feel a lot of love for your cooking, then the dinner tastes great. But if you're resentful and tired, then you'll find dinner doesn't turn out as nice. It's the same thing with finance. With a dash of passion, we can cook up a storm with both our food and our money!'

We need simple, digestible solutions to get back on track. So in this book, we're going to break down the ingredients for good money management and see what can happen with the right ingredients.

Creative cooking

Getting to grips with your financial position involves more than just filing a tax return on time and putting money away into an online account. It's about knowing what you want to achieve financially and when, and how you'll do it. How do you want to live? What do you want to do with your money? Get creative.

Saving and investing doesn't have to be a boring or time-consuming activity that will zap you of energy. You don't need motivation or interest, you just need a wish list and some ideas about how to be creative with money, and feelings like motivation and interest will follow. Acting your way into a new way of thinking can be the first step towards a goal. Don't let your feelings be the guide, Dorothea advises.

First, write your wish list—your goals, your financial 'menu'. Ask yourself: 'What do I want my life to be about?' For example, you may want to have enough money to go on two holidays a year, eat out three times a week, have the occasional beauty treatment, and save a bit for a rainy day or an emergency. Knowing what you're aiming for is crucial. Without an incentive, you have no reason to stretch yourself and your motivation will be low! We'll look at setting goals in more detail in the next section.

If one of your wishes is to own your own home, decide how much money you should save. Where do you put those funds in the meantime? Should you buy a property to live in or as an investment; which is better? We'll cover the pros and cons of various investments in later chapters.

Next, the essential, basic step for all astute money cooks is to divide up your money — a good rule of thumb is to save 30 per cent and use the remaining 70 per cent for living. The savings money is then divided again into short-term and longer term funds: the short-term funds for play money, the longer term for super and investing.

The next step is where the creative part comes in, courtesy of Dorothea: reframe your savings/spending mix in the language of something you're passionate about. Reframing allows you to look at something that you consider negative in a different light. When you view things negatively, you tend to feel threatened and avoid taking action. By reframing them in a more positive or realistic way, you're more inclined to deal with them. So, if you're a gardener, you could picture having different pots to plant your money in and watch it grow and bloom, like flowers. Some flowers can be picked and placed in a vase — that's your play money. Then there are the annual flowers which bloom once a year and the perennials which bloom twice a year, giving you returns to replant or reap.

If you like reading or writing, you could relate types of books to different aspects of money management. A shopping guide book could mean money for spending. The rare books that are locked away and rarely touched might translate to savings—something that will keep growing in value just like rare books do. Your normal living expenses might equate to your must-have books to read and the blockbuster novels stand for a holiday account. Since food and finance have underpinned my working life, I've chosen to use cooking as the main metaphor throughout this book.

Make sure you put yourself in the mix, too, Dorothea says! Avoid pigeonholing yourself and using your personality to explain away bad habits or procrastination, even if it explains some of your behaviours, inclinations and dislikes. Instead, consider what you value and try and use that to help you manage your money. In other words, align the 'real you' with your financial goals.

Your cooking style

One of the most important things to understand about the 'real you' is your attitude towards risk. Higher investment returns carry a higher risk; lower investment returns carry a lower risk—you need to know what you're comfortable with. (Investments that appear too good to be true, by the way, are just that!) Every time you invest, you take a risk, whether big or small, that that investment may:

- not do as well as alternative investments
- not do as well as other investments of its type
- be performing poorly when you need to sell it
- not earn enough even to keep up with inflation
- make a loss and reduce your capital.

The quick questionnaire that follows will help you become more aware of what drives you—your values and behaviours—when it comes to money.

Quiz: Understanding the financial you

My approach to life is:

A Take no prisoners. I'm very positive and throw all my energy into everything I do. Some say I'm reckless. I say I'm driven to succeed.

B Focused. I have a strong and clear idea of where I'm going and what I want to achieve personally and financially. Things generally work out well for me. Friends say they don't know where I find the time.

C Considered. I weigh up the advantages and disadvantages before making decisions, but when I do act, I do so decisively.

D Agreeable. I like getting along with people and prefer to seek consensus rather than risk making the wrong decision alone.

How important is getting ahead financially for you?

A Essential. I work very hard and pump as much excess income as possible into making more money. That means making some lifestyle sacrifices in the short term, but it will pay off.

B Very important. I have a weekly budget, set strict financial goals and stay focused on building my assets. But I make sure there's still enough for restaurant meals and a trip away each year.

C   I'd like not to worry about money, but my lifestyle and happiness mean I sometimes live from pay packet to pay packet.
D   I'd like to be a bit better off, but having a happy and fulfilling life is what inspires me. Money is only a means to an end.

Thinking about your investing experiences, would you say:

A   I love it! I've made a bundle and see opportunities to make money everywhere. I reckon I understand investing and do all my own research.
B   I enjoy it. I've done well with most of my investments, though there have been a few failures. I read widely and seek advice.
C   It gives me a headache. I have sometimes listened to the wrong people and haven't had as much success as I would have liked. Perhaps I don't have the time or knowledge to make the most of my money.
D   My investment experience has really only been in fashion. I know a little, but I've never really been able to put extra aside into investing.

My attitude towards taking financial risks is:

A   Yes, please. If the potential return is high enough, I'm prepared to lose money four years in every seven, so long as I come out well in front. I'm open to most things—nothing stupid, though.
B   I understand risk, so I look to balance higher risk investments with less risky ones to ensure I don't lose out overall.

C   I'm more concerned with stability, so I'm not really interested in taking too many risks. I'm okay with some shares, but blue chips only, please.
D   Risks? Nope. No thanks. Not interested. Slow and sure is the right approach for me.

When I invest, I put my money away for:

A   As long as it takes to get the return I'm after. I'm happy to trade shares every day and rebalance my portfolio frequently just to make sure I'm ahead of the game.
B   The medium term. I don't like locking my money away forever, but short-term investments just seem too volatile for my comfort.
C   About a year. I want stability and surety over market peaks and troughs that cause me stress and fear. And I want to be sure that I can access it if I need it.
D   The next sale at DJs. I really can't afford to have my money locked away out of my reach. What happens if I have an emergency?

So who are you?

Mostly A   The Warrior. Adventurous, active, positive and aggressive financially, but may need to better balance the risk–return equation.
Mostly B   The Manager. Financially aware and adept, and seeks information before acting. But are you overexposed if markets fall?
Mostly C   The Traveller. Understands a bit about money but would rather go along slow and steady with investment than accept high risk. Could you be doing more with your money?

Mostly Ds The Lover. The financial fear factor takes a back seat to making sure life is comfortable and predictable. Things seem okay now, but consider taking more control to ensure things can grow and improve.

© Evolution Media. This quiz is for entertainment value only and should not guide investment decisions.

Financial planners like to assess your risk appetite by talking about your finances passing the sleep test — if you don't wake up worrying about things when the going gets rough, you can probably handle a higher risk level! If you spend a lot of time stewing over money, you may prefer sticking with conservative investing choices, such as cash management trusts, a home mortgage or managed funds in blue-chip shares.

On the other hand, if you've bought high-growth assets such as shares in the past, and found that this worked for you, you may like to look into leveraging your investments.

Keep in mind that a big event like divorce or the arrival of a baby can change your risk outlook. Some of our case studies also show that people tend to prefer lower risk investments more as they get older.

Choosing the menu: goals

When you're writing your wish list, try to project the big picture for the next decade. Remember, though, that your goals and priorities will shift as you move into different stages of life. Be flexible about where you're heading, and adjust the list as circumstances change.

In your twenties, you're full of hopes and dreams and busy trying out different experiences and buying possessions.

The savvy are already saving and researching investments; the not-so-savvy are in debt. Credit can be a big trap at this age: it's easy to rack up high mobile-phone bills, take out personal loans for holidays and cars, and max out the plastic.

In your thirties and forties, you hit your career stride and have a greater earning capacity. You may find yourself thinking more about saving and putting down anchors: getting a mortgage, for example. You may also have kids, with all the accompanying joy, angst and expense. If you're childless, you're in the sweet spot of your earning capacity. You can really focus on what you want to go for.

It's worth noting that people in their twenties, thirties and forties are generally classified as 'accumulators' or wealth-makers by financial advisers. However, women's working lives tend to be drastically affected by having a family. Your peak time financially *should* be middle age, but that's not always the case. If you've separated from a partner or sacrificed your career for the sake of the kids, you may hit leaner times in your forties and fifties. Still, seek out whatever opportunities you can find within your current situation! Here are some simple suggestions for each age and life stage to help you kick-start the goal-setting process.

In your twenties: eat now or eat later?

- Consider your career path and how to make the most of work and increase your income over the next five years. Relocating to another state, or even overseas, may help improve your financial position.
- If you're in your early twenties, try saving for a short-term goal like a car or trip. Work out how you

can save $100 a month or $25 a week in order to save up $1000 for the year—you can do it! Debit the money out automatically before you spend your pay. Also, have a go at keeping the occasional month-long spending diary to track where your money's going.
- Take financial stock. Internet-based investments can be attractive to this age group: shop around for high-yielding online accounts or managed funds, or start building a share portfolio.
- Look carefully at your credit-card use and avoid getting into uncomfortable amounts of debt. Try a charge card with an interest-free period. Drawing out cash advances is the first sign of big problems to come!
- Think about raising a deposit for your first property— sometimes this can be kicked off with a family gift. Consider investing with a friend or partner.

✱ Janelle Diprose, 29, IT professional: 'When I returned from living overseas last year, I was very conscious about my financial wellbeing. I began earning a comfortable income and wanted to "settle down" financially. Until the last 12 months, I was earning to spend on travel. Now, I have a mortgage with a partial investment property, a high-interest savings account, and am about to invest in shares with my tax refund'.

In your thirties: salad days

- If you haven't already in your twenties, at this stage you may have to save for a wedding or a baby. Think about

how you'll afford six months to two years off work if you stay at home with the baby, or how you'll cover childcare costs if you go back to work quickly. Then there are the kids' education costs—average private secondary school fees add up to $100 000 over the six years.
- Other short-term goals could be upgrading your existing house and car or funding your own business.
- Look at your spending and savings program, and see if you can make enhancements. This is a time when your cash flow may be really squeezed, and that can affect your ability to get loans. It's also very easy to be a spendthrift at this age, given all the needs and wants that come with it.

※* Jo Cowling, 34, has worked in Sydney's real estate scene for over a decade. She came to fame as a *Biggest Loser* contestant in 2006. Last year, she says a close friend helped her reassess her spending, and she took on a 'substantial' property mortgage:

'I've never been a goal-setter. Now, I realise the importance of goals. I want to be financially secure—I don't want to be dependent on someone else, nor do I want to have to struggle. I'm only now putting things into place to ensure this. I wish I had done it sooner...hindsight is always is a wonderful thing! I like to have fun and be generous, but one of my best girlfriends taught me a new mantra: "Is this getting me to where I want to be?" It's important to look at the long-term and not just the short-term joys'.

✱ Cathy Charnley, 39, contractor and mother of two boys: 'We've had a wish list for the past four years. I've already ticked off renovating the house, having children and buying a business. We want to go overseas, but that hasn't happened yet since we work demanding hours. The new goals are buying a bigger house and having the second child, which happened early this year. Having a cleaning business has made me appreciate money more; you need to think ahead and put money aside for different reasons, such as saving for the new baby and medical costs'.

In your forties and fifties: is it cooked yet?

- It's time to look hard at your retirement plans. You'll need at least $500 000 in your superannuation kitty at retirement to achieve a 9 per cent return — an annual income of $45 000. (That's regarded as an average benchmark, but whether it's realistic depends on your spending patterns.) How many years of income-earning do you have left to generate this before age 65? How much more can you salary sacrifice or put away? Use the calculators at <www.fido.gov.au> to get a rough idea.
- Review your financial resources overall. Now's the time to seek financial advice with the long haul in mind.
- Fulfil some short-term personal goals — maybe study, or travel? You may also want to change direction in your work life or pedal back to part-time work. This is a great time to reinvent yourself!

✳ Susan, 43, divorced with a young son: 'Being a businesswoman, I'm good at cash flow but not at lifestyle finance. Recently, I wanted buy a new car after my lease ran out leaving $20 000 to pay off — not a lot. I pay myself $150 000 a year, but because I'm 43 years old with no house and a slender amount in the bank, I was unable to get the loan. That surprised me! We all labour under the idea of marrying and being happy ever after. It's an evil myth. I wish I'd squirreled more money away'.

✳ Marie Farrugia, 45, presentation coach and mother of one: 'When my son was two and a half, my mother had a stroke at age 57, and that was a shock. She survived, but her quality of life went down. It really made me look at my own life and question what I was doing. I also thought about the bigger picture regarding money. I said to myself that at age 50, we will have a choice whether we work or not…Now I'm 45, and I think [that goal's achievable]. A year ago, we started up a self-managed super fund, which was another tick off the goal list'.

✳ Susan Ross, mother, midwife, businesswoman and author of *Birth Right*, recently sold her family home and decided to rent in order to free up some money to put into the business:

'Property is my main area of interest. I've done three [houses] so far. The last one I lived in and stayed put for three years. I borrowed a lot and the bank balance did go down during that time. Now I'm child-free, animal-free and debt-free...

'I'm renting, but my aim is to get a new property in the medium term. I've never been without a property in Sydney—I could get quite distressed about that. I've got a limited amount of super because I've been a contractor, so property has been quite important to me, as well as working in the business'.

What's in the pantry? Your net worth

After you've got a wish list and a new frame for your basic savings plan, you need to open the pantry doors and see what's in there—in other words, you need to calculate your current net worth. 'Net worth' may sound stuffy, but it boils down to what you own versus what you owe. One of the easiest ways to do this is to take the free wealth test at <www.wealthbenchmarks.com.au>, which will give you a comprehensive report on your financial position and how it compares to others in your age bracket, life stage and profession.

Seeing how you stack up financially against others can be very helpful. Many women hitting their thirties, forties and fifties feel they should be further ahead of the game when it comes to assets and wealth. But are they being realistic? The comparison figures in a Wealth Benchmarks report will help answer that question.

Knowing your key financial ratios—such as your loan gearing ratio, your debt-servicing ratio and your savings ratio—can also make you feel differently about where you stand. It's not just about lifestyle. You can appear rich yet be debt-ridden. You can be cash-poor and asset-rich, but if your debt levels are in hand, that's fine. You can be cash-poor and asset-poor. That's tough, and climbing out of that state takes effort—but it can be done!

> Katrina Pulbrook, an ANZ Financial Planner, warns: 'Beware of debt. People who have the look of wealth may have the most debt. Often, the house is the essence of your net worth, but it's still all about cash flow. Loan-to-valuation ratios should always be checked—because if you don't have enough money, you will have to earn more [to meet payments]. You probably don't want to sell a property too early, because it takes seven years or more to be worthwhile. You want to cash in on the growth; usually, it's expensive to get into the asset initially.
>
> 'Super tends to be neglected when purchasing a home and when parents are busy paying off the school fees. A lot of people want their kids to have a private education but haven't prepared for it financially. Sometimes, parents fund the kids' fees through the home mortgage and choose to go back into debt. But that's at a time when they should be thinking about saving up for later! It's easy to put off starting a savings plan, but if you leave it too late then you have to put more in to top it up. And time marches on regardless'.

We all know that money is a means, not an end. Your net worth acts as a reference point for how you're tracking towards your financial goals. Maybe it's not something you like to think about much or discuss openly, but it's a useful figure to assess yearly. Your long-term prospects for independence will flourish if you take the time to think about your finances more often!

Other people's pantries: Lucienne

Lucienne Francisco is an innovative chef whose CV includes time as an apprentice at the acclaimed French Laundry in California. In three short years, Lucienne and her husband (also a top-rated chef) have built a good financial position for themselves through the purchase of a small cafe in Avalon, New South Wales, the Chelsea Tea House, and a property. In order to buy the Chelsea, Lucienne borrowed money from her parents, and their house was purchased with a bank loan:

> We came from the US with savings, but had very few assets. We got a loan [for a house] because of my husband's job and locked in the loan at 6.2 per cent…While it's a great thing to do, it's also meant that the bank wouldn't extend credit on my business. I'd have to break the loan to get an overdraft, and I'm not willing to do that! Anyway, it's our first house and I'm ecstatic when we make mortgage payments. It's such a sense of accomplishment. I feel I should have had this a long time ago!

Like many cafes, the Chelsea runs on a tight margin. The costs are high: Lucienne follows the principles of the Slow Food and sustainable food movements, and is proud of her ingredient quality. She favours organic, seasonal produce, which tends to be more expensive—and there's not much in the way of GST credits for it either!

Net worth: Lucienne

Assets	
House and contents	$1 200 000
Car	$40 000
Business	$200 000
Super	$10 000
Total Assets:	**$1 450 000**
Liabilities	
Mortgage	$700 000
Overdraft	$120 000
Total liabilities:	**$820 000**
Net worth:	**$630 000**

She comments:

> There are a few cafes in the precinct and it's very competitive. Just getting through the first winter in the business was hard, and I made the mistake of not saving enough from the peak summer period...plus we needed new furniture and a new awning sooner than I thought.
>
> Then, during this summer, I was down by 20 per cent on my revenue because we had crazy weather and the surf was very cold, which affected the holiday-makers. But we were up on our revenue for the year as a whole.

Looking at the 'pantry' makes me feel like I've accomplished something. But it's also scary to carry that kind of debt that can only be paid off by the house or the sale of the business, or if we get a lot busier — a bit precarious, I know, but I suppose that with a father who is an entrepreneur, that kind of risk has always been part of life. He's earned and lost millions several times over, with our family moving up and down, in and out each time.'

Time to start cooking

After you've thought about your financial style, made your wish list and calculated your net worth, achieving your goals is about taking small steps over time — consistent, persistent effort really does pay off! We'll look at the nitty-gritty of managing your money over the next chapters.

Simple beginnings: Jo Cowling's Thai chicken + lychee salad

480g chicken breast fillet, cooked and shredded
20 fresh lychees, peeled, deseeded and halved
  OR 425g canned lychees, drained
1 small red onion, thinly sliced
8 spring onions
2 cups bean sprouts
½ cup well-packed mint leaves, torn
½ cup fresh coriander leaves, washed

Dressing
1 tsp finely grated lime rind
1 tsp sambal oelek
¼ cup lime juice
1 tsp sesame oil
1 tbsp sugar or sugar replacement
2 tsp fish sauce

Combine dressing ingredients in a jar and shake well. Combine salad ingredients and pour dressing over just before serving.

Chapter 2
Cutting Back on Sweets

> I went to an all-girls' school and I think I had bad spending habits even then!
> —Bella Serventi, former *My Restaurant Rules* contestant

Are you a big spender? A shopping addict? Or a careful keeper of the purse? You don't have to be extravagant for everyday purchases to be running your life and limiting your future opportunities. Cutting back on spending can be the way to save, just like cutting back on sweets can help you become healthier. If you have more money available, then you can put more aside — it's obvious, yes? Hell, no!

The reality is that most of us love shopping more than we love not spending. There are some things in life, such as a good cappuccino or a shoe or homewares hit, which can feel indispensable. Even if you hate the hell of a busy shopping mall and prefer funky boutiques or department stores, shopping can take you into another zone and offer an escape from the responsibilities of home and work. You don't have to be a Kath or a Kim to appreciate that! Janelle, 29, admits:

> I'm a big spender. I'm an impulse shopper. I love coming home with bags of shopping, but I also

chastise myself for being overindulgent, because I shouldn't be spending the money.

Dorothea explains that the urge to splurge is about feeling good and, sometimes, about social standing:

> [But] instead of feeling good, women are over-buying for the buzz and end up feeling worse. It becomes a vicious circle when it happens too often...You need to get into the practical zone (Do I need it?) and out of that emotional zone (I've had a tough week!).*

It's not just women, of course. The funny thing is that while women are often very conscious that they're frittering away their money, men can spend up big on bits and pieces and be totally unaware of it. A Virgin Money survey confirmed that, on average, men spent almost $3400 a year on discretionary items like lottery tickets and takeaway food and drink. And men earning $40 000 a year spent almost as much as those earning over $70 000 a year. The yearly averages for both men and women make for interesting reading:

Where the money goes

	Men (p.a.)	Women (p.a.)	Total (p.a.)
Takeaway drinks, food and snacks	$2168	$1539	$16.53 bn
Magazines, lottery tickets, etc.	$598	$458	$4.72 bn
Little luxuries—taxis and dry-cleaning	$629	$317	$4.23 bn
Total	**$3395**	**$2314**	**$25.47 bn**

© Virgin Money

Because it's easy to pay on credit for immediate gratification, over-spenders risk becoming 'debt collectors'. Ask yourself:
- Are you shopping when you're bored or depressed?
- Do you feel excited when you contemplate spending?
- Do you often feel guilty about your purchases?
- Do you find yourself buying things that you don't need or really use?
- Do you find that when you get your purchase home, you don't want it?
- Do you buy things you can't afford?
- Has your spending increased?
- Do you often spend more than you intend to?
- Do you save money, then spend it all in one big splurge?*

* From 'The Money Pit' by Julianne Dowling. This material first appeared in *Notebook:* magazine, August 2006, p. 93.

If you're over-spending, try charting an emotions map of when and where your sprees occur, and then work out some strategies for dealing with them. Here are a few different ways to avoid the sugar high of unnecessary spending:
- Become aware of your financial situation; for example, the balances of all of your accounts.
- Write up a saving/spending plan that details what you owe now, how it will be repaid, future costs and how much you'll put aside for savings (a holiday account, super, a rainy day stash?).
- Record everything you spend in a small notebook that you take with you everywhere.
- Don't take your credit cards shopping—use cash.
- Write a shopping list before you leave the house and stick to it.

- When buying gifts, decide on the maximum amount that you can afford and stick to it.
- Wait at least 24 hours before making any purchase.
- Put items on hold if you really like them, but don't put any money towards them.
- Enlist the help of a supportive friend—someone you can confide in who's a careful spender and is happy to tag along on shopping days as the voice of reason.

Take one day at a time, and don't beat yourself up if you slip. We all have setbacks; the important thing is to keep trying. If you're struggling financially, think about getting help from a professional to work out your relationship with money and spending.*

* From 'The Money Pit' by Julianne Dowling. This material first appeared in *Notebook:* magazine, August 2006, p. 92.

Beware the silly season

At Christmas, I used to go overboard and spend $500 on my nieces. Now, I'll lay-by presents and only buy for the younger children.
—*Cathy, 39, contractor and mother of a two*

Christmastime is a killer for splurges in both food and money, especially for those blessed with a big circle of family and friends. According to 2006 Sensis data, the average Australian buys 10 presents worth about $857. Worse, according to a Virgin poll in 2004 one in four shoppers buy 'one for you and one for me' presents! Another money pit is food and drink for Christmas dinners and parties—a 2006 Australian National

Retailers Association survey says we spend 25 per cent of our budget this way. Holiday travel and fun spending are other danger areas.

You don't have to spend a bomb at Christmas to show you care—just buy thoughtfully. It can also help to set a dollar limit on gifts in your family or circle of friends in advance. You might even agree to give the money you'd usually spend on presents to charity for the year. And, of course, sometimes the best gifts are the ones you make yourself—over the years, some of my arty friends have become expert giftmakers. Having the kids draw all the family Christmas cards and wrapping paper is another good tip. It's charming and will save you instant bucks. At $4 a pop, a nice card can be a wallet-whacker!

Counting kilojoules: budgets

> We had to budget when things were tight and I hated it. Now, we don't really do it consciously at all.
> —*Shwei, 46, mother of two and student*

Love 'em or hate 'em, budgets are useful. But unless you've run into major debt—when changing spending habits and sticking to a budget is essential—budgeting can seem like a big blah!

But becoming conscious of your spending patterns, even for just a few months, can be a real eye-opener. Understanding where you're spending can help you realise what you value and assess whether you're spending in line with those values. For instance, do you value education? Are you putting money into training, workshops or your children's schooling? If you feel you don't have the money to spend on education, yet you're spending a lot on clothing and looking fashionable — and that isn't as high on your values list — then you immediately know where you can cut back!

Unless you get motivated about your long-term values, a budget can feel restricting. If you know your values, setting a budget can actually feel liberating — it becomes a tool to help you achieve what you want, not a punishment. Don't beat yourself up about your spending habits, just look at your situation and resolve to try out some different approaches. And start now, today! If you're tempted to put off taking action, Dorothea has this to say:

> Recognise your sources of procrastination. Do you have negative thoughts or fears about your ability to manage money, for example? Or are there external causes, such as making money decisions to please others rather than doing what's good for you in the long term?

Budgeting isn't just about cutting back on expenses: it's about organising yourself and your money. Keep it personal and use a goal — 10 per cent is often held up as a good figure to reduce your spending by and funnel into saving and investing. As with all goal-setting, it helps to work on this with a coach or a like-minded friend. Rope in a mate, set a savings goal each and encourage each other to stick with it.

Don't forget to reassess your budget and goals regularly, too, as your spending patterns will change, and to allow for irregular spending on things like medical and dental costs and extra gifts.

Financial planner Delma Newton, founder of Total Portfolio Management, says it takes a shift in mindset to make budgeting work. Once it's under control, though, people learn to manage their discretionary spending better:

> Usually, we put people through budgeting for two months and track all expenses for four weeks. We do a budget and reallocate the surplus to paying off debt. Most people are back on track in three to four months. It takes discipline, because they've been spending freely, and [they need to make] conscious decisions such as choosing between going out for a few drinks or sitting at home. It can be very confronting — often people feel guilty about being busted!

A healthy diet

Georgia Henry, a drama teacher and mother of three, finds the 'obsessive, Depression-style' saving hints popular on the internet — such as living on $20 a week and then using up the pantry food — hilarious. 'Yep, here's the answer to our budgeting dilemmas: soap bits in pantyhose!'

There are less radical tactics within reach for producing a financial surplus. Maybe it's giving up one weekly DVD hire, pooling magazines with girlfriends, buying one less bottle of wine each week or washing the car yourself rather than shelling out $10. That's at least $40 in savings a week — $2080 in a year. Let's take a quick look at two couples and how they're managing to save without depriving themselves.

Budget #1: no kids

Account manager Georgie, 29, is totally committed to building a deposit for her first home with partner Ian, so budgeting is top of mind. But she still loves her holidays and overseas travel! The couple's expenditure works out to roughly $5726 a month, but they're saving heaps. Their largest spends are on entertainment and travel. Here's what Georgie spends in their key areas and how she's made cuts:

Georgie

Bills

Household bills (e.g. phone and internet):	$60 per month
Mobiles (2):	$120 per month
Electricity:	$60 per month
Gas:	$50 per month
Total:	$3480 per year

Saving strategies

- Phone bill—For international calls, phone cards are great. We pay for our internet and home phone through our ISP: the call charges are cheaper.
- Mobile phones—One is used for work, so we claim it on tax each year. Prepaid can be good; also, we shopped around for good deals and plans—cap plans can be great if you have a regular phone usage.
- Electricity—We get our bill monthly rather than quarterly, for two reasons. One, it's not one big hit every three months, and two, it's an average of usage, so you can end up paying a bit more in the first two months and having a small amount in the third month. Also, we use energy-saving bulbs, turn lights off and all that good stuff…

- Gas—Gas is cheap for our hot water and stove, so short of ceasing showers and cooking, saving is not an option really!

Public transport

Taking the bus to and from work:	$17 per week
Total:	$884 per year

Saving strategies
- We purchase 10 tickets at once for $16, saving $1 a week.

Entertainment

Daily coffee:	$20 per week
Eating out:	$100 per week
Drinks at a bar:	$50 per week
Takeaway once a week:	$20 per week
Work lunches:	$60 per week
DVD purchases:	$60 per 3 months
Books:	$300 per 3 months
Total:	$14 440 per year

Saving strategies
- Coffee—I cut my coffee from two purchases daily to one, and drink the free office-supplied tea during the day, saving $20 a week.
- Eating out—We go out for dinner once a month rather than once a week now. Our friends rotate having dinner parties instead, because all of us either have mortgages or are saving for one!
- Drinks at a bar—Again, this is now usually once a month. If we do go more often, we try to catch happy hour and then either head to someone's house or to dinner.

- Work lunches—A major cost! We now cook extra dinner meals and freeze them or take salads, and only buy one lunch each a week.
- DVD purchases—We don't hire DVDs; we buy and lend them among friends, which splits the cost almost by half.
- Books—We do the same with books as with DVDs. It cuts the cost by about a third, as I have a group of three friends to share the cost of new books with.

Holidays

South-East Asia once;
interstate twice: $9000 per year

Saving strategies

- We book international flights early through a reputable travel agent. Good travel agents can tell you when taxes will increase; they can also organise the cheapest way of getting visas and so on.
- For domestic flights, we get online for Virgin Blue's daily sale hour, which can save you lots.
- The web is great for finding international hotel deals, but it's very seasonal and sometimes you can get a better deal through a travel agent.
- We joined groups like YHA to get discounts on travel-related products like vaccines and backpacks.
- Sites such as <www.wotif.com> are fantastic for domestic accommodation. Book at the last minute and you can save up to 50 per cent.

Financial costs

Credit cards, etc.:	$50 per month
Accountancy:	$150 per year
Bank fees:	$10 per month
Total:	$870 per year

Saving strategies
- Credit cards—The credit card I have is linked to Frequent Flyer and is my only form of debt.
- Bank fees—We use only our bank's ATMs. When we get a home loan, we'll also cut down on bank accounts; currently Ian and I each have one everyday and one savings account. We also have a high-yield internet account for savings. We'll consolidate our separate accounts once we get a home loan and set up all our legal agreements.
- Super—We're trying to consolidate all our super into a single fund. Trying to get an exact figure from the existing super funds (I had three) was a nightmare!

Private health insurance
Total: $1800

Saving strategies
- I had a lot of dental work done recently and the amount I got back covered my premiums; now I'm reviewing my membership. I aim to get a cheaper policy with ancillary cover on optometry and dental work to avoid the Medicare levy.

Savings
Total: $1600 per month

Saving strategies
- We use a high-interest account to avoid fees and get the best interest rates, and have our money debited out each month so we don't even notice it. At the end of each month, with all that we've saved, we put half into savings and half towards a special treat or splurge.

Yearly total (including costs not listed here): $87916

Budget #2: a family of three

When children come into the equation, there's a lot more pressure on the money flow. There's the cost of education, the kids' living expenses, childcare fees and, of course, added stress on accommodation—you may need to buy or rent a larger place for your growing brood, not to mention their stuff! Your holidays also become more expensive, as you're limited to peak periods. Even if you can go off-peak, your destinations may be restricted by the size of your entourage.

Jenny and Simon* have been spending around $9400 per month, but they want to make cuts, as they recently decided to purchase a negatively geared investment property (a property for which the rent won't cover the mortgage), which will mean going from nil debt to mortgage payments of $2800 per month. The family's largest expenses are their two motor vehicles, entertainment, outsourced help and insurance. Here's their plan for saving:

Jenny and Simon

Motor vehicles (2)

Insurance:	$2000 per year
Registration:	$1000 per year
Fuel costs for Jenny:	$50 per week
Fuel costs for Simon:	$100 per week
NRMA memberships:	$160 per year
Car servicing:	$2000 per year
Total:	$12 960 per year

Saving strategies
- Avoid unnecessary and long road trips.
- Use fuel vouchers from Woolies and Coles.

* Real names withheld on request.

- Try to buy petrol early in the week when prices are cheaper.
- Target savings: $1100

Entertainment

Two daily coffees:	$42 per week
Eating out/takeaway:	$150 per week
Work lunches:	$50 per week
Total:	$12584 per year

Saving strategies
- Consider buying a coffee machine for home.
- They can't do without the weekly takeaway, but they can cut the restaurant trips to once a week.
- Target savings: $100 per week or $5000 per year

Outsourced help

Cleaners:	$140 per month
Fortnightly mowing:	$65 per fortnight
Garden clean-ups:	$350 per quarter
Quarterly window wash:	$160 per quarter
Pool chemicals, cleaning and maintenance:	$200 per month
Total:	$7810 per year

Saving strategies
- Reduce all outsourcing, especially on the pool.
- Target saving: $2000

Personal insurance

Life, disability and income-protection insurance for Simon:	$10500 per year
Income-protection insurance for Jenny:	$3000 per year
Total:	$13500 per year

Saving strategies
- In Jenny's words, 'No savings here, because as you get older switching policies may not give any real benefit and you may lose cover. If you're debt-free then you may consider whether you still need a high level of insurance, but if you still have a young child then best keep it going!'

Other insurance

Home and contents insurance:	$1200 per year
Landlord's insurance:	$380 per year
Private health insurance:	$2500
Total:	$4080 per year

Saving strategies
- The couple checked with their insurer for help on average prices in their area. (You can also check with Master Builders Australia.)
- Annually review private health insurance premiums at <www.iselect.com.au>.

Yearly total (including costs not listed here): $113116

A 10 per cent saving: $9900

Actual cuts: $7420

Budget versus cash flow

Cash flow isn't the same thing as a budget, points out Louise Brogan, financial coach and founder of All Money Matters: 'A budget on its own doesn't ground people in the reality of their living and spending habits'. Going from full-time work to freelance, part-time or casual work can be a challenge, because a downsized income doesn't guarantee downsized spending habits! If you're planning to take a break, start a business or downsize your cash flow, it can be a good idea to do a dress-rehearsal for the change and spend as if you are earning less. Keep a diary of your daily spending to analyse your patterns and see how you go on a reduced income. For example, if your partner works and you're intending to have a child, try living off one salary for three months or so before you stop work. Automatically debiting money into super or a savings account is a good way to cut your cash flow and do some saving during the trial period.

When opera singer and producer Ali McGregor left a lucrative career at Opera Australia to go out on her own, she says the first victim of her reduced cash flow was her savings:

> When I was on a regular salary, I saved every week into a high-yield account to build up money for a deposit. But after I went freelance, my savings went out the window because it's hand to mouth.

Ali bought MYOB software in order to better organise her business and personal accounts, and takes a DIY approach to all her shows to cut expenses.

> I design everything, including my website and posters. I like that I can do it myself, and that's why I don't lose money. I source my costumes from second-hand stores and eBay, and I have a few beautiful things like corsets that I love. I'm a thrifty spender; I do make purchases now and then and, of course, some I can live without. But I don't go crazy—some of my friends have $15 000 credit card bills! I could do better. I lived

on a budget when I had a regular salary coming in, but now my life is too erratic. I just try not to spend too much. Being part of a couple has changed things: my partner earns more than me and it took him a while to convince me that I didn't have to go dutch. I've eased up on that; I try and make up for it in other ways like cleaning the house and doing the washing. I like a certain quality of life, but I don't need masses of money. I'm not interested in having things as much as doing interesting things.

Tax-wise

Here's another way to save: pick up lump-sum refunds from the taxman at year end by keeping all the right receipts and knowing your entitlements. Check the Australian Taxation Office (ATO) website (<www.ato.gov.au>) on what's relevant to your occupation — you might discover new claimable items or higher caps on claimable items. Keep in mind that if you claim more than $300 in total on work-related expenses, you need to be able to justify them with receipts.

Accountant Michelle Pearce, director of Face Chartered Accountants, adds that taxpayers often forget to make the most of tax offsets to reduce their tax bill. It might be a good idea to check with your accountant about the medical expense offset (the total amount claimed back from medical expenses) and offsets relating to child care.

On 1 July 2007, the Child Care Benefit went up 10 per cent — a family on the maximum rate with one child in long day care for up to 40 hours a week will receive an extra $16.40 per week. The existing Child Care Tax Rebate, which covers 30 per cent of your out-of-pocket expenses up to a maximum of $4000 plus indexation, has been converted to a direct payment. You can claim it as a lump sum or a weekly discount.

Getting out the preserving jars

So you've gone through your spending, worked out what to cut back and set a budget. Is achieving your goals just an automatic debit away? What's the best thing to do with all that extra money? Let's have a brief look at how two high-flyers salt their savings away before we move on to take a look at taming credit cards in the next chapter.

* Peggy Barker, co-founder of Barker Wealth Management: 'A powerful way to save is through regular automatic debit. You can start off with smaller amounts if you go into managed funds rather than direct shares initially. If you want to keep it really simple but flexible, you may consider friendly society bonds directed to Australian shares and/or fixed interest. These bonds can pay tax at 30 per cent on their earnings, so all bonuses and growth in unit prices are tax-free after 10 years. Generally, withdrawal in the eight and ninth year may attract some additional tax or rebate, depending upon your personal tax rate'.

* Linda Coates, Masu Financial Management: 'I put at least 10 per cent of my net income towards

wealth building—and that gets harder with the kids and their needs—but the aim is to lock it away through automatic debit. I also pay extra on my mortgage...and I have a credit facility on it that I can draw down, so I can release some of the investment's equity. You need cash flow (mostly through earned income) to do that. Understanding and creating cash flow is paramount'.

Healthy eating: Ali McGregor's braciola

Hammer a Scotch fillet steak to within an inch of its life—as thin as possible without tearing it. Then sprinkle it with fresh parsley, crushed garlic, breadcrumbs, parmesan, and salt and pepper to taste.

Roll the meat up and skewer it with a toothpick to keep it together. Pop it under the grill on medium heat until the top is browning and slightly crisp. The Braciola should be very tender inside and a little pink. Yummy, healthy and a very quick dish.

Chapter 3
Out of the Frying Pan

> *I tend to use credit cards and then pay back when I have the cash.*
> —Kirsty Brooks, author of seven books, including *The Lady Splash*

You don't want to be a broke gal; you certainly don't want to be a down-and-out one either! The celebrity-spending culture among under-35s has meant unheard-of bills are racked up on plastic. In a bid to emulate the stars, hair, make-up, accessories and fashion all become must-haves—86 per cent of younger women (and almost half the blokes) say they feel they should match the designer wardrobes and idealised images of the rich and famous. Two out of three women accordingly pull out their cards and spend up large. Haven't we all been there at least once (and sometimes back again)?

Having said that, most people like credit cards and find them manageable. According to the Reserve Bank, the average debt for cardholders between 18 and 64 years of age is a tad below $2600, with younger people having slightly higher balances.

The celebrity spender's shopping list

	Women 18–34	Men 18–34
Clothes and accessories	64%	64%
Grooming and make-up products	44%	26%
Haircuts and styling	37%	31%
Beauty treatments (e.g. facials, manicures and fake-tanning)	26%	11%
Gym memberships and personal training sessions	13%	22%
Cosmetic enhancements (e.g. teeth-whitening and Botox)	7%	7%

© Virgin Money

Interestingly, credit agency Veda Advantage points out that over a five-year period women were less likely to default over credit cards, mortgages and five-year loans than men and more likely to pay their bills. Women made up 38.6 per cent of total defaulters on credit cards. Members of generation Y (those aged 18 to 27) were responsible for a third of all defaults in 2006. (In 2006, 3.7 million cards were applied for, and a third of applications were made by that age group. The number of credit card applications grew by 7.3 per cent and personal loan applications jumped by 8 per cent in the same period.)

Traditionally, cards have come in two flavours: charge cards with membership fees that must be paid off monthly (or you get hit with penalty rates) and credit cards with monthly ongoing balances that have an interest rate attached.

There's also a few new breeds of 'pay now' cards: debit cards that draw down from your existing cash account, prepaid cards and debit/credit hybrids.

Cleaning up the kitchen

The trigger for people to fall into deeper debt is often an inability to meet repayments on multiple cards. A 2005 survey by the Institute of Chartered Accountants found that consumers with three or more cards had an average debt of $4387, compared to $1183 for those with only one card.

Reward points on credit cards work like cheese for us mice, but can you afford to take the bait? Don't overspend and justify it with the idea of free flights and treats. Sure, you can get those tickets to Singapore—but it'll be at the expense of your future wealth!

Changes to outstanding balances are another minefield: be conscious of the interest rate you're paying and the fees charged. If you've gone for a 'zero' or low rate of interest, be aware that any repayments may be taken off that low-rate balance first, leaving you with new purchases being charged at a higher interest rate. Reviewing your credit card and charge card spending regularly makes sense—and online tools make it easy to compare different cards. Useful sites include <www.infochoice.com.au>, <www.artog.com.au> and <www.cannex.com.au>.

Paying off your existing credit card balance using a new card that has an interest-free honeymoon can be a helpful strategy. There's a huge trend towards 'migrating' to low-rate cards for this reason. Just be aware that too much card-hopping could give you an unsatisfactory credit rating; zero-rate and honeymoon-rate cards may also charge higher interest on repayments or late payments than your old card. Merryn, 31, a nurse, made sure she avoided this trap:

> I moved my credit card balance to one that had a six-month interest-free period and then worked to pay it off in the six months.

Freelancing and its accompanying cash flow problems is another factor that can make it difficult to resist the tempting push and pull of credit and debt. Adelaide 'chick-lit' author Kirsty Brooks is no stranger to the financial famine/feast of a creative life. As well as relying on a credit card to tide her over, she counts her blessings that she has a supportive partner to cover any shortfalls until the royalty money comes in:

> I think the financial situation has always been twitchy in my industry. I'll get a pretty big cheque, which would be great for saving or putting down as a deposit for a house, but I end up using it to pay off the bills from the last quarter.

Kirsty is disciplined about her work and sets goals, but admits she's never been considered the 'sensible' one in her family:

> I'm not all that great with money, [although] I always have a one-year and five-year plan for my writing. I think sometimes those things are so drilled into you that you live out the role of being 'non-sensible' (i.e. hopeless) at things because you think that's your role. I'm good at some things: I can write the hell out of a

love scene and send favourite characters to a hideous death—but money? Not my forte. Sadly.

Basic recipe: credit cards

- Pay more than your minimum, or you'll never get rid of the debt.
- Understand the fees during and after the introductory offer period.
- Find out the fees if you exceed the spending limit.
- Check the repayment or late payments policy so you don't end up paying more than you thought.

Source: <www.artog.com.au>.

Putting credit on your shopping list

Petrina Milas, a make-up artist, coach and stylist, was watching *The Oprah Winfrey Show* and was so impressed by a strategy that helped viewers ask for a better deal from their card providers that she decided to give it a go herself.

Petrina, whose clients include TV personalities and dignitaries such as Rudy and Judith Giuliani, uses her credit card to buy stock for her studio in Northbridge, New South Wales, and occasionally for travelling, so it's a valuable business tool. Petrina is keen to find new ideas and tips for saving money, which is why the *Oprah Show* caught her eye.

> They talked about how Americans could go to their credit card providers and pressure them to cut their rates. They even had a script you could use, so I

downloaded it and rang my own card company. They wrote back and said they were 'glad' I asked and gave me a reduction!

After that experience, I urged my husband to contact his card provider and ask for a rate review on the rolling balance on his card. Initially, they resisted, but we asked to speak to the supervisor and they responded by saying that if we transferred the amount on my card balance to their card then they'd cut the rate down to 6.99 per cent for the life of the debt. We were staggered, because the rates had been in the double digits. So it really pays to try this approach! We'll keep looking at our money situation to see how we can improve it, but this certainly is a good start.

I…think you need to get the whole family on board with money management, and successful families do talk about it more frequently too. For example, I was doing make-up for a woman and her husband was there discussing their savings goals with the children, and I thought that was great.

Finance comparison site <www.artog.com.au> highlights that some cards will grant you an annual fee waiver if you spend between $5000 and $10000 annually. You can also ask for a relationship discount—lower fees and charges in return for consolidating all your business with the one institution. However, this is not a green light to go out and spend more!

Also, make sure you check how your credit card's interest rates are calculated. In early 2007, a report from consumer watchdog *Choice* found that up to 10 different methods were used to calculate the interest due on credit cards and that you could be paying double compared to other cards!

The health inspector's report: your credit file

The first step towards a healthy credit file is to apply for your file in order to know what lenders are looking at when they assess whether or not to lend you money. Financiers are not obliged to tell you the reason you've been declined finance. Veda Advantage (formerly called Baycorp Advantage) is the leading credit agency and it has relationships with every credit provider. You can order a copy of your credit file from its website, <www.mycreditfile.com.au>; it costs $27 including GST for delivery within one working day, but if you can wait 10 days it's free.

If you have an overdue account on your credit file (these can be listed if the account or payment is 60 days in arrears), it'll stay there for five or seven years unless you take action. Prior to listing, however, the credit provider must have taken action to collect the money, such as sending you a letter to let you know that the payment is in arrears. Credit providers can also extend the time before they list the account as overdue at their discretion.

To fix up your file, you need to square your debts with your creditor and then contact Veda to make sure that the file is updated. Once your file is clear, it can be helpful to check it every year—or if you prefer, you can ask Veda to send you email notification when there are any changes on your file—this service costs $30 for 12 months.

'Most lenders are quick to clear up any problems', says Veda's Kristen Boschma. 'But unfortunately, most Australians don't know that a credit file exists on them and how banks and other credit providers, such as mobile phone providers, go about their decision making. It's important to know what's involved in credit applications so you can be aware of the process. By monitoring your credit file you can also protect yourself against identity theft'.

It's an important point—the incidence of identity theft is on the rise. A lot goes undetected, too: the first sign may be a lender telling you that you're in default on a loan that you didn't take out! Apparently, identity theft often starts with mail theft—thieves get copies of your bills, bank statements and other identifying documents and use them to replicate your profile. They may also go through your bins for documents. Veda's advice is to keep your mailbox locked. If you live in an apartment block and there's a bank of mailboxes, it's even more important. Other tips are:

- Shred all paperwork such as bills and bank statements.
- Sign your credit cards as soon as you get them.
- Store copies of your cards in a secure place and keep another set of copies elsewhere—maybe in a bank-deposit box or at your parents' house.

Case study #1: wedding cake blues

Habitual spenders aren't the only ones who can find themselves in debt that's hard to handle. It's easy to get into trouble at points in your life when there are big outlays, such as a wedding or the arrival of a baby.

Like many young couples, 29-year-old Jo Atzori and her partner are building their lives in a sensible way. Jo says she's a good saver and her husband, who works for a bank, is fully aware of the importance of having goals set for different intervals and then working out a plan on how to get there.

The trouble is, while they're paying off their mortgage, they're also loaded up with HECS debt and are paying off a credit card bill and finance on their car and furniture. The couple managed to save around $8000, but this was spent on their wedding in the Whitsundays.

> In the past year, my husband and I have only paid off a very small part of our home loan because the majority of our payments meet the interest. If I could change my financial situation, I would change the amount of debt my husband and I currently have.
>
> Still, before I met my husband, I didn't use a budget. I now have a monthly budget in Excel, where I enter in the amount I get paid along with the taxes and super. From the amount left over, I list all my monthly expenses — although the unforeseen expenses sometimes muck it up.
>
> My view on our financial position is 'Wow!' because if you'd seen us five years ago, you'd be astounded at how far we've come. I had no job and was living off $320 a fortnight on the dole. My husband was earning half of what he earns now and we had nothing. A $10 pizza was a big investment for us. The sky's the limit if you really work out what you want to achieve and do your darnedest to get there!

Jo's main goals are to stick to her monthly budget and pay the bills. Other short-term goals include saving up over a few months for a weekend away for her husband's birthday. Their medium-term goals include having finances in place for when they have a child in a year or two and setting up an education fund when the baby arrives. Another medium-term goal was recently met when the couple sold their townhouse and purchased a new four-bedroom home. Their long-term goals include having enough super to retire; they'd also like to travel overseas over the next 10 to 15 years.

What Jo and her husband can teach us:

- Apart from trying to reduce your interest rates, budgeting is the *only* way to stay in control of multiple debts.
- Goals are a brilliant way to stay with the big picture.

Learning more about money management has really helped Jo, and she hopes that other young women can see the value of getting back to the basics of saving, budgeting and having clear goals.

Case study #2: kitchen disaster zone

Sometimes, things go off the rails completely. For Laura,* a mother in her thirties, the spiral of debt started when she stopped work to look after her two young children. Her story began innocently enough with one credit card. Then she applied for a second card and, after spending more than she could repay, got a consolidating loan to pay both cards off. At that point, the loop should have closed — the cards should have

* Real name withheld on request.

been cut up and the loan repaid. But they weren't, and a bout of retail therapy pushed her back to square one. Frightened by her situation, she started to let the other bills go, things quickly spun out of control and the creditors began to move in to retrieve their funds. This time, she was drowning in debt and scared about the reaction of her family—she feared it would unravel her marriage.

There's no doubt Laura had gone through a bad year. Her family were grieving, she'd been plagued by flu and depression and, not surprisingly, this flowed through to her job. But she moved to fix her problems. She cut up her cards after the second lapse and worked out a repayment plan for her creditors. Here, she tells how she tried to get her situation back on track.

> I was about $30 000 in debt from credit cards, a personal loan with a high finance lender, a huge mobile phone bill, massive gas bill and unpaid rates. One credit card company garnisheed my wages, so I fell behind in my house payments, which never happened before. I tried to keep in contact with all my debtors and work out payment plans and was okay until the garnishee of wages occurred. Then I was totally lost.

Laura was so upset that she took a very brave step and posted on *Notebook:* magazine's online forum asking for advice on how to recover.

> I don't want to sound like a victim, because I got myself into the mess, but I was floundering and didn't know which way to turn. I tried to apply for personal loans,

but no normal lender would even look at me because of my impaired credit rating. I even approached the 'non-conforming' bad debt lenders, but they only wanted to refinance my home — and this was not an option, because my house is in joint names and this was not a joint problem. I felt totally alone.

The forum members urged her to contact a free emergency financial counsellor — these counsellors advise people who've become enmeshed with multiple cards when bankruptcy may be the only way out. They also asked her to consider whether she could earn more money, but the stress of her situation was making her feel so ill that it wasn't possible to take on more work.

The upshot was that Laura was told by the counsellor that she needed to act fast. Since the credit cards were the most expensive debt, they had to be repaid. The loan was the second priority. The garnishing would pay down one card over two months, but what about the other debts?

After more negotiation, the other card company agreed to ease up on repayments. She also sorted out her priorities — shelter, food and family, and then the creditors — made a budget and stuck to it. A few weeks later, she paid off her first credit card, her mother helped her out with bills in arrears and she started working two part-time jobs to pay off the other debts. A month later, she finally told her husband about the problems, and they separated.

Six months down the line, however, Laura is exuberant. After a few weeks apart, she and her husband worked through their issues — and more importantly, Laura was able to build up her sense of self-worth by taking charge of her money, working full-time (which she enjoys) and losing a fair bit of weight. For some women, it can take an 'Aha!' moment to really make a difference; for Laura, the separation was it. Being able to survive all these challenges has convinced her that she is her own woman and can deal with them.

> I've paid back one credit card and have almost paid another one. By the end of this year I'll be debt-free. I've lost weight and I am feeling and looking fantastic. My secret? I took responsibility for my mistakes and started to add some control to my life.

Laura has two essential tips to moving forward:

> First, I keep a journal for each payday up to four pays in advance (I get paid fortnightly). I write down every bill that needs to be paid and add up the total. Anything left over is a bonus, or I can pay other incidentals. This is the best thing I could have done, because I can see what needs to be paid in black and white and I'm keeping a record as well.
>
> Second, I opened an internet banking account and set up direct debits for bills. Each fortnight, two days before I get paid, I log on, check my journal for what bills need to be paid and make sure these payments are scheduled to be automatically transferred to the billers when I'm paid. This has been a godsend, as I don't have to make a special effort to go somewhere to pay my bills—it's automatically done each pay. The beauty of internet banking is that you can

change payment amounts from fortnight to fortnight according to your budget.

All Money Matters' Louise Brogan sees many women in debt; here are her comments on the situation of Laura and others like her:

> The worst thing to do is to try and wish the problem away! It sounds logical, but it's surprising how often people go into denial and do nothing. Acknowledging your creditors is vital: they're so much more likely to assist in a debt repayment agreement when they know that they're being taken seriously and included in the process. Until your money problems are acknowledged and faced, nothing, I repeat nothing, will change!
>
> Laura should be congratulated for taking that first step and contacting someone qualified to help. This doesn't mean that you [shouldn't] get support from friends or family (if that works for you and is appropriate), but working with an independent professional is the key to turning your situation around.
>
> It's a sad fact that those who have financial problems in this country can be isolated and judged by the public at large. When our business and political leaders are telling us we've never had it so good, suffering financial hardship is even more difficult to come to grips with. However, there are fabulous support networks like DA (Debtors Anonymous) and financial counsellors, and they're often free.

Once you've connected with professional help, please, work with them to face the reality of your current situation, identify what went wrong and make sure you change your habits so it can't happen again.

Many people who come to us are brilliant at paying off their debt, but end up right back in debt again and again. Why? Well, this behaviour—the constant indebtedness—is something they know and understand. It's familiar territory. No-one showed them how to change or break those old patterns.

Even when they've worked out a new system, some people find it extremely difficult to stay with it. To make it easier, the system must be simple and take away the need to be constantly making decisions—'How much will I spend on fares/food/clothes this week/month?', 'How much can I save this pay?', 'What should I set aside for the bills now?' So much energy is taken up by going through this each payday!

So, what are the steps? Louise advises:
- Admit you have a money problem.
- Get good help from a financial counsellor or coach.
- Work with your counsellor or coach to put together a cash flow plan and, from that, a spending plan that includes debt reduction and repayment.
- Identify the things you did that went wrong, and learn from them to change your behaviour and systems.
- Give yourself time for your plan to work. As you can see, Laura only started seeing significant results after

six months. Depending on the depth of your problem, don't expect changes in anything less than that period.
- Keep it all very simple. Get rid of your credit card — use debit cards instead.
- Get ongoing support, especially when you've reduced or paid off your debt and want to start saving and investing. This is when those old sabotaging habits can kick in and take you back to square one!

Good luck and enjoy the journey!

Cheap and tasty: Kirsty and Mark Brooks's vegieburgers

The burgers
1 large tin of canned tomatoes
1 large tin of chickpeas
2 carrots, finely grated
3 zucchini, grated, with the liquid squeezed out
1 cup cooked fresh corn or canned corn kernels
4 onions, grated
1 clove garlic, mashed
2 teaspoons each of cumin, turmeric, garam masala and any other spices you like
pinch of mustard seeds
2 eggs
flour
breadcrumbs

The rest
any soft rolls you prefer
Beerenberg tomato sauce to taste
lettuce to taste
sliced tomato to taste
fried egg to taste

Mix all the burger ingredients together except for the eggs, flour and breadcrumbs. Add these until the consistency is right—soft, almost sloppy, not solid. The mixture should initially stick to the spatula when you throw a clump into the frying pan and flatten it.

(cont'd)

Kirsty and Mark Brooks's vegieburgers (cont'd)

Cook burgers slowly until one side is light brown and then turn. Bits will fall off, especially chickpeas, but the consistency is such that you can squish them back on again. It's not meant to hold together, as too much flour or breadcrumbs will take away the slightly spicy taste. And it's okay if the middle stays soft. Just cook them until they're ready (I like them sort of burnt…), then serve on a roll with your favourite burger ingredients.

'We created this recipe while sharing house together, being vegetarians and not having much cash', says Kirsty. It's a great, messy, super-tasty meal, even if you're not vegetarian!

Chapter 4
Beyond Home Economics

> *Yep, having a home... it's a nice feeling. I feel like a pretend adult!*
> —Bianca Dye, radio star, author and TV celebrity, on buying her first home

What is it with chicks and bricks? Why do we like the idea of property so much? Are women hardwired for property ownership more than men? No less than 70 per cent of women say they'd rather own property than shares or funds, believing it to be a safer investment and one they can relate to. Despite the lack of affordability in certain cities and suburbs, many women also remain interested in direct property because of the 'touch and feel' aspects—it's not an abstract investment like shares. This is a dish in your cooking repertoire that you can get your fingers into! The rising rate of home loan approvals for younger women suggests a trend towards increasing ownership (Wizard Women *her homeownership* research report, 2006).

Not surprisingly, though, there are still many women who find the thought of taking on a mortgage quite daunting and not really *them*. Luckily, there are many paths to property. Instead of taking out a mortgage, you could invest via a listed property company, an unlisted property fund or a property security fund. It comes back to knowing yourself and your objectives, your ability to handle risk, your time frame for any investment or major acquisition, and your financial circumstances.

If you plan to buy and this is your first time round in the market, the biggest hurdle is to get that big lick of money together for the deposit and additional costs. It's not easy. A survey by Mortgage Choice in December 2006 revealed that about 62 per cent of people said they found it harder to save for a deposit compared with 12 months previously due to rate rises—and since then, further rate rises have meant they need to save even more. Choosing to buy means deciding that you're prepared to limit your lifestyle in order to save, and being certain you've got the discipline to make those monthly or fortnightly payments after the purchase.

Shopping for property

Your grocery list

Property-finder and expert Nicole Graham knows what makes a property special—she's spent a decade finding clients' dream homes in her work as a property search consultant. She says some buyers spend far too long searching for perfection:

> People need to open their minds! If the property meets 70 per cent of your requirements, then work on it, but if it's only ticking 60 per cent of the boxes, forget it.

With a first home, you need to consider how your life will change in the next five years and whether the house will still suit you in the long term. Location is also critical—when a suburb takes off, the price rises in good pockets can double compared to the bad pockets. So, don't just look at the average percentage increase of a suburb, but which pockets increase and whether the property is close to good features like green space and water.

Nicole also points out that the location of a home is even more important to women than to men because of women's lifestyle and safety requirements. A single woman, for instance, has to consider whether an inner-city apartment is secure and well-lit at night.

Scarcity is another factor that has a big impact on price. Houses on, say, Sydney's Balmain peninsula are likely to increase in value faster than units because houses can be knocked down and units built.

Nicole's shopping list

- Find a juicy location, squeeze out the good areas and discard the bad bits (the bits with traffic noise, lousy neighbours, industrial sites, speed humps).
- Set three budget levels ranging from a comfortable level to your absolute limit.
- Buy in the best position that you can afford.
- Make a list of your objectives.
- Talk to people you know who live in the area to find out what's good and bad about it.
- Check with the local council about upcoming nearby developments. You don't want to find

out too late about the planned multi-storey building that will block your view!

When you find a property, look at the demographics. Is there a good tenant pool? Does the neighbourhood fit your profile? Do your inspections reports and don't ignore the bad bits — these are negotiation points! — then get the contract checked by your solicitor. Don't make your first offer your last offer unless there's a very, very good reason.

Property trends in Sydney

- Unrenovated properties are less popular than two years ago.
- Buyers are more conscious of space and are buying in outer suburbs to get more space.
- Indoor/outdoor space is more important.
- Flashy kitchens are less important.
- Seventies architecture is more popular.
- Proximity to public transport counts for more.

Source: Nicole Graham, Ray White Real Estate Newtown.

At the checkout: the mortgage

Experts talk a lot about affordability — the amount of income you have to commit to the monthly mortgage repayments — but that's not the only factor to consider when you're deciding on a mortgage. Lisa Montgomery, Resi Mortgage's Head of Consumer Advocacy, says there are five things you should examine (in no particular order): interest rates, fees, the loan's features, the flexibility of the loan and the service from the lender.

Interest rates are a no-brainer (see <www.infochoice.com.au> and <www.ratecity.com.au> for comparisons between lenders). These days, you should get a loan without ongoing charges—you may be able to negotiate away the annual fee. Features such as offset accounts, card access or redraws should be part of the deal—if you don't want too many features, you may be able to get a cheaper rate. Flexibility [is important]. Can you fix the rate, get extra funds and move the loan around to suit your changing needs? Service-wise, you need to be comfortable with the person you're dealing with. Are they providing guidance on maximising the loan so you can pay it off faster and possibly make savings? Ask the questions in advance and don't wait until it's too late!

Lisa adds that you need to look at the annual percentage of interest, the fees and any costs if you decide to pay the loan out or redraw funds. This information is in the loan disclosure document.

Given the high levels of competition for customers, there may be gimmicks on offer, but free plasma TVs, travel and petrol shouldn't sway your decision on the right deal for you. The newest mortgage product is 100 per cent loans. Remember, the provider takes their cut of any capital gain when you sell, and there's a hefty interest bill tacked on. Low doc loans are popular with borrowers who don't have proof of income, assets or liabilities, and tend to suit the self-employed and women who have had periods out of work. However, the interest rates and fees associated with these loans tend to be more expensive. More experienced investors are also exploring direct online mortgages—'no frills' products that can potentially save on fees and rates. Whatever type of loan you choose, always, always make sure you can meet the repayments comfortably, with a margin for rate increases. Mortgage Choice's 2006 survey showed that women were less confident than men when it came to covering higher payments from increasing interest rates.

> ✳ You only need $2500 to buy a $250 000 home in a cheap suburb or a regional town—you just need to qualify for the First Home Owner Grant and be able to repay the loan. Be aware, though, that credit card limits will be counted in your loan application and you'll be offered a sum less the total card balances, even if you don't actually owe anything on them.
>
> But did you know that a lender can insist on mortgage insurance where the deposit is less than 20 per cent of the total price? That'll add an extra $3000 to your expenses. And mortgage insurance is for the lender's protection—not yours!

Fees and discounts

With any purchase, even after you've stumped up the deposit you'll possibly be facing a mortgage establishment or loan fee (usually about $600); service fees (which can be thousands over the loan life); inspection costs; and legal and valuation fees (usually about $200, although if you're lucky, they can be part of the loan fee). And if we say the average Sydney house price is around the mid-$500 000 range, then stamp duty will be around $11 000 for first-time homeowners and about $20 000 for others. This varies from state to state, of course.

On the plus side, the Commonwealth Government's First Home Owner Grant provides a one-off payment of $7000 that isn't means-tested or restricted by a purchase price threshold—check <www.firsthome.gov.au> to find out if you're eligible. Each state has its own variations. For example, the New South Wales First Home Plus Scheme provides eligible purchasers with exemptions on transfer duty and mortgage duty on homes valued up to $500 000 and land valued up to $300 000. New South Wales also grants first-home buyers concessions on duty for homes valued between $500 000 and $600 000—though you need to apply through an approved lender if you need this money at settlement.

In New South Wales, the state government also allows concessions on shared equity loans. A purchaser taking a 50 per cent share in a $500 000 home, for instance, will qualify for a $9865 stamp-duty discount. Residents of Victoria may qualify for a state government cash handout. In Queensland, a number of concessions are available on mortgage duty, but get in soon, as these will be abolished on 1 January 2009.

Garnishing: renovation

If you're renovating a home to live in, you can pretty much do as you please. But if you're renovating to sell, Nicole recommends you don't spend more than 2 per cent of the property's total value on renovation and focus on the smaller kitchen and bathroom improvements. Maybe add a new splashback or a new double sink instead of a single sink, and upgrade the old formica benchtops with stone ones. A quick and effective way to revamp cabinetry without replacing the doors or units is to add funky handles.

Backyards are important because they really do give more resale 'oomph'. Lush turf is a good investment to add kid-appeal, and planting two large colourful trees at the rear of a basic block will enhance the perception of space. As a general rule, Nicole recommends spending between 1 and 2 per cent of the property value on landscaping and plants. If your place is in the inner city, a Jacuzzi or a well-designed barbecue on the balcony can be a good way to appeal to the 'funky crowd'.

Nicole's renovating recipe

To one property, add a dash of revamped kitchen and bathroom. Keep an eye on the renovation budget as a percentage of the total price of the property, and don't forget the outside. Returf your scraggy lawn or add a smart barbie on an apartment balcony, and you'll get more $$$.

Shopping while hungry: Bianca Dye's story

Bianca Dye is one of Nova FM's top-rating radio stars, an excellent multi-tasker and a creative force who's co-authored a book with Dr Cindy Pan about modern relationships (*Playing Hard to Get*, HarperCollins Australia, 2007). A dog lover, Bianca has three canine friends (her two elderly dogs loathe the new kid on the scene, a Kelpie cross!), so it's no surprise that she also appeared on the *Celebrity Dog School* series. Bianca's major asset is her inner-city house, which she bought almost four years ago. She has some regrets:

I jumped into buying the house too quickly. Being single, I was up against couples with money. I had a budget and kept missing out at the auctions. Mum's a real-estate agent in Queensland and she was advising me, only it was all by phone. Once I missed out on a house I adored to a couple with far more to spend; I found myself crying in the car later, which shocked me because usually, I'm pretty tough. In the end, I bought a house that was exactly to the dollar of my budget; it's cute, two seconds' walk to Newtown and has two bedrooms.

I love this house, but I paid top dollar for it and I'll have to stay in it forever before I get a profit...Now, I'm living here with my boyfriend...We need a bigger kitchen, so I'm going to gut it and fix it up. Our mortgage is $3500 a month and by the time I pay my bills, my pay is almost gone...what I earn extra outside of radio is my living money and the house is my savings. The house could rent at $450 a week, but I'd still have to find the shortfall for the repayments.

Discounts and hidden extras: Rachel Thompson's story

Last year, Rachel Thompson, 32, bought her first home with her husband, Michael. They'd strolled past the three-bedroom apartment in the street where they rented on Sydney's lower North Shore a few weeks before auction. Though the owners wanted more than the couple had in mind and they hadn't done any inspections, the agent suggested that they attend the auction anyway. Rachel went along on the night and kept Michael informed by phone. Surprisingly, their offer of $500 000 was accepted after the property was passed in. Rachel was thrilled.

> It's a very spacious apartment built in the 1950s. Afterwards, we wondered if we paid too much, but then looking at other property results since the auction, we know that's not the case.

That $500 000 was the threshold purchase price needed to qualify for the First Home Owner Grant in New South Wales and get the full stamp-duty exemption, which meant a hefty $20 000 discount off the sale price.

> We'd saved a little over $75 000, including $12 000 from our family. We're in a position to pay off a quarter of our mortgage in the next few years. If we do decide to start a family, we could get by on one salary.

But buying a property isn't just about the purchase price — payment shock starts with the extras:

> Because this was the first time for us and we hadn't been seriously looking, we hadn't thought about things like settlement and legal fees. In the middle of all this, my husband's mother unexpectedly passed away. We just had to drop everything and fly back to the US. We had to manage and find the additional money, since almost all we had was going on the settlement.

When we moved in there were other costs besides the furniture movers, such as changing the locks and putting up insect screens. Even with my husband doing it himself, it still cost us a couple of hundred dollars. We will repaint, recarpet and eventually put in a new bathroom. The kitchen is fine for now, and we like that the dining and living rooms have timber floors. I think it was just luck at the end of the day; we think the sellers really needed to get rid of it.

Resi Mortgage's home loan recipe

Want to pay off your property faster? Resi Mortgage says that the seven steps are:

- making small extra repayments
- making more frequent repayments
- salary credits
- lump-sum repayments
- taking advantage of interest-rate falls by maintaining payments
- getting to know your loan's features
- giving priority to the debt.

Sharing the goodies with family and friends

Baby boomers tend to have a lot of money tied up in their family homes while their kids are struggling to raise a deposit. To help their kids buy property, they may wish to pool resources. Joint family ownership can also be a good option where one family member would find it difficult to shoulder the load of a mortgage on their own.

If you're thinking of taking either of these routes, however, it's important to have a legal agreement in place to cover the ownership structure (whether you're joint tenants or tenants in common); the disposal of the property; and issues relating to rent, upgrades and maintenance. You may have harmonious views initially, but 10 years down the line, your needs and goals may be very different!

Research commissioned by Wizard Home Loans reveals that the main concerns of people who pooled funds included disagreements about selling (31 per cent) and worries about the other borrower being unable to meet the repayments (23 per cent). These are problems that can be avoided if a legal agreement covering the role and responsibilities of all borrowers is in place before you get the loan.

At 29, Janelle Diprose returned from living overseas and wanted to 'settle down' financially. She invested in a freestanding property 20 minutes from the Melbourne CBD with her parents, who were looking to move there from South Australia. Her parents live in the property as their primary residence, and Janelle invests into it.

> My parents suggested that we buy a place when they moved back to Melbourne. It's on the cheaper side of town, but it's already worth more. We've renovated the pool and landscaped it, and we're looking to do more work on the property. They couldn't afford it alone and neither could I. So it works out well. We each have a third share, with a 10-year plan for holding the property. They may buy me out…it depends. But we're all committed to it. They still have their original home and have rented it out. So they've still got a

rental property and share the mortgage on the other one with me. I have other siblings, and I worried about what they'd think. But my eldest brother was really happy about it. I guess I'm the transient member of the family, and maybe he saw the move as a good thing. I'm chuffed about that.

Cooking for one again: property after divorce or separation

Women who have split up with their partners often want to use the settlement, if it's substantial, for a property. If you're investing into your home for capital gain (and it's tax free) then that strategy may serve you well. However, many financial planners believe that this isn't a good call if you're going to struggle to meet the payments or if there's a huge amount of equity tied up in the house. If your immediate need is for cash flow, then you might want to consider looking for an investment that gives you an income stream instead.

For many women, though, owning their own home is paramount after a divorce or separation, regardless. Sandy* recently bought herself a two-bedroom semi in Crows Nest, New South Wales, costing $800 000, and is convinced that the purchase was right for her.

> We put a lot of work into the former family home in Perth. I had my daughter there and when we split up and sold it, I rented in Perth for 12 months and

---

* Surname withheld on request.

then in Sydney for 12 months while we sorted out the settlement. From 19, I've always had property and I felt that was the best option for me — I don't regret it.

We've been here (in the new house) for four months and it's been very consolidating. Long term, it will be a good investment and it's capital gains tax–free. We could invest in the sharemarket and maybe get a higher rate of return, but it works better for me this way. I know after two years of renting, and feeling like I had no [permanent] place, settling back again is very satisfying. I felt like I was home again.

Cooking for profit: property investing

Investment properties aren't a get-rich-quick strategy, as property tends to work in longer cycles than other types of investment. It depends on when in the cycle you buy or sell. Time it wrong and you can lose money! Furthermore, negative gearing (offsetting the deductible expenses of the property against your income to lower your tax) is becoming less attractive, with interest rates rising, property values stagnant and the thresholds for personal tax rates rising.

Property also carries risks, just like any other investment, and finding ways to minimise the risks is vital. Choosing good property managers and tenants is one way to reduce risk. Understanding your state's tenancy laws, researching the vacancy levels in your chosen suburb and obtaining landlord's insurance are some other ways to protect yourself somewhat.

At 52, health-worker Rose Elliot Jones had jointly owned two residential properties — the first in Melbourne and the second in Tasmania. However, a serious setback on the second house and a split relationship meant a forced sale. She's had to virtually start all over again raising money for a third place—without the benefits of the First Home Owner Grant or other exemptions. She's in a quandary about the headaches of home ownership, but doesn't want to keep renting into her old age.

The first property in Victoria was jointly bought and sold, and the sale went smoothly, with a good profit. This funded the next joint purchase of a large bed and breakfast house and business in Tasmania. Because it was a big eight-bedroom heritage-style house, it carried more costs. Rose says she and her friend lived in it and ran the business for a while, but then they decided to move to Sydney and rent out the house. That's when her troubles began.

First, Rose says she couldn't find a reliable property manager, and she shifted from manager to manager, hoping to find a better deal.

> The difficulty was that the house was never expected to be a rental property. There's a lot of unemployment and the house attracted larger families who were often out of work; it wasn't in a good part of town, so that was an issue.
>
> Having tenants turned out to be pretty awful; I'd never recommend it. I had a manager for a while and the tenant moved out after smashing things up but it was six weeks before the agent sent them a letter. Later, I sold for a loss—$10 000—maybe not a lot for some, but it was frustrating.

Rose has saved $30 000, with a target of $50 000. She's looking at a budget of $150 000 to spend on a cottage in Hobart: 'The end game is to get somewhere to live and make the best of it. It just means starting all over again.'

Property management

Not everyone is able to manage their own investment property. Distance and other factors may mean a professional manager is the only option. Property managers collect the rent, pay the quarterly outgoings, then disburse what's left and take an average 7 per cent of the gross rent for their services. They also select tenants, do inspections, report on and maintain the property (you may elect to authorise emergency repairs up to a preset amount, perhaps $500), and act as the link between you and the tenants.

Real-estate agent Terase Calligeros has investment properties of her own. She advises that the negotiability of the agent's fee depends on how many properties you have with that manager; how long you've been a client; the quality of the property; and how much the agent wants to manage it. She warns:

> Document everything, because there's always some turnover in managers. And don't bargain the property manager down too much on their fee, because you get what you pay for. Having a good rapport with the manager is essential, as is knowing that they'll respond in a timely way to requests. Maintaining the property is really important—a bit of paint, carpet replacement and yard-clearing can help attract quality tenants.

Terase Calligeros's agent recipe

Choosing an agent? Here's a handy checklist of questions to ask:

- What's the ratio of staff to properties?
- How many properties do they manage?
- How quickly will they inform you about repairs and maintenance?
- Will they notify you about repair quotes beforehand?
- What's the turnaround time for repairs?
- Who do they use as handymen, plumbers and gardeners? Ask to see the list and check how long they've been using them.
- How frequently do they inspect a property? Quarterly or every six months? Usually, there are ingoing inspections and regular inspections thereafter so when there's a changeover of tenants they'll occur more than once a year.
- Can you have a carbon copy of the inspection report, so you can keep a running record of the state of repairs and ongoing repairs?
- Will digital photos be kept as records before and after tenants come in?

Source: Hamilton & Co, Terase Calligeros

Insurance pays off

Terri Scheer, an insurance broker in South Australia, comments that she often hears investors talk about 'good tenants', but that even with the best of tenants bad things can happen. It may be that the tenant decides to do a weekend paint job on your precious property—in puce! Specialist insurance covering damage and accidents can really help, she says, along with keeping up with any new laws, like the upgrade in the glass standard on any window replacements.

> It's a good idea to consider a smaller property in a sought-after suburb when it comes to tenants. There's less damage with solo tenants, and sometimes the returns can be just as good on a two-bedroom compared to a three-bedroom place. However, single tenants may also sublet rooms to friends without the landlord's knowledge, so taking out insurance is a must even if it seems like dead money.

Investors with holiday-let apartments can also get landlord's insurance with public liability cover, but insurers generally won't cover them for disrupted income due to an insurable event. Though this can be arranged if you can prove the income attributed to the rental, it may be subject to dispute come claim time for holiday-let premises.

Having your cake and eating it

Horticulturist Bettina Class, a single mother with two children, chose to take a different route: she bought a rental property while continuing to rent herself. This decision was partly driven by limited funds, but it's worked out very well. Bettina is renting a lovely bungalow owned by her aunt in a beachside suburb that's been her stamping ground since childhood, and she loves it.

She's used her savings, plus some funds from her family, to invest in one of the fastest-growing places for property values—Broome, Western Australia. Her property is in Roebuck Estate, a suburban development, where in 1997 land was offered for sale at $50 000 a block. At the time of writing, it had three-bedroom houses valued between $560 000 and $600 000 and renting at $500 per week. New-release blocks start from $354 000 and go up to $428 000 in the exclusive areas. Even Landcom blocks, which are sold on a ballot system, start at $200 000.

Be warned, though: Broome is booming just now because of the mining industry, but it may not last forever. Before you rush out to buy a place there, take care that you're not buying into the peak of the cycle—do your homework! Bettina got in relatively early and snared a block of land with a house for around $265 000, borrowing $156 000. With high rents another feature of Broome's boom, she's 'Stoked!' She adds, 'Another year and the property will have doubled its price. The prices have gone up so much I couldn't afford to buy it now'.

She's also fortunate to have scored a rental contract with a government department, which gives her some peace of mind regarding the tenants.

Getting the government to buy your cake: negative gearing

At this point you may be rolling the words 'negative gearing' around your mouth and wondering how this much talked-about approach might work for you. To explain the concept and its pros and cons, we've called in a professional—Michelle Pearce, director of Face Chartered Accountants. Here are Michelle's wise words:

Negative gearing is a familiar concept, but few people really understand it. It all seems simple enough—buy the right property and then have the tenant and the Australian Taxation Office (ATO) partially fund your repayments while you sit back and profit from the appreciating property value. However, is it really that easy to make money? And if not, what are the factors people need to consider when investing in property?

The ATO provides a tax incentive to property investors by allowing them to offset an income loss (where property costs are higher than property income) incurred on a real-estate investment against any other income.

Let's look at an example. Say that a taxpayer is earning $50 000 per annum (plus superannuation) and is thinking about purchasing a property for $188 000 (inclusive of $8000 in purchasing costs). She has managed to secure a loan with a bank, borrowing 90 per cent of the property value on a 25-year principal and interest loan with a current fixed interest–only rate of 7 per cent per annum. She makes weekly loan repayments in advance. The developer has offered a five-year rental guarantee at $250 per week. The rates and body corporate fees total $2000 per annum and the rental management commission to be paid is 6 per cent.

We have also assumed annual depreciation is $1500 (remember, this is not a cash outflow unlike the other rental expenses). At the end of the first year, the profitability of the taxpayer's property investment would be as follows.

Rental income	$13 000
Rental management	($780)
Loan interest	($12 600)
Rates, etc.	($2000)
Depreciation	($1 500)
Total	**($3 880)**

	Taxpayer with no property	Taxpayer with one property
Salary	$50 000	$50 000
Property tax loss	—	($3 880)
Taxable income	—	$46 120
Tax and Medicare levy	($11 100)	($9 878)
Net income	**$38 900**	**$36 242**

As you can see, a rental loss of $3880 has had an after-tax effect on the taxpayer's net income of $2658 ($38 900 − $36 242). In this scenario, the tenant and ATO actually fund the annual property costs (remember the depreciation expense of $1500 is not a cash outflow, thus the cash rental loss is $2380).

It should be noted that this won't be the outcome for every property investment. In some scenarios, a property can mean a net outflow of cash, where the tax benefit is less than the net cash rental loss. This means you would need to fund the investment and hope for an appreciation in the value of the property to cover the costs. This may be difficult if you buy at the peak of a property cycle.

Keep the following in mind when assessing such a situation:

- Is the building on the property new or old? If it's a new property (that is, recently built) then you can claim 2.5 per cent of the cost of the building as a depreciation expense. This is quite an advantage and was one of the key assumptions in the above example. Please note that you will pay tax on 50 per cent of the depreciation claimed at the time you sell your property, assuming you hold it for more than 12 months. This is because depreciation of new buildings reduces the cost base of the property when you calculate your capital gain. However, a permanent deduction for 50 per cent of the depreciation is clearly still an advantage.
- For there to be a benefit of negative gearing, you need to continue to work and earn income. A rental loss which cannot be offset against other taxable income is just a loss at the end of the day.
- For how long do you want to hold the property and for how long can you afford to hold it? You need to consider these issues because if you buy a property at the 'wrong' time, either because it

was the peak of a cycle or when interest rates were rising, then you need to be able to afford to keep paying the bills while you wait for your investment to appreciate (assuming it does).
- Don't just buy a property because of its 'tax advantages'. A negatively geared property will make an annual loss, so you need to make sure the potential capital gain is realistic.

This is not an exhaustive list, and you should seek financial advice before making an investment in property.

Other tax deductions or implications to keep in mind:
- If you decide to rent out your principal place of residence and rent a place to live yourself, then you're still eligible for the principal place of residence exemption if you either move back into or sell the property within six years from renting it. This means you should not pay any capital gains tax on the sale of the property for the period it was rented.
- In addition to the normal annual costs of having a rental property (such as advertising, rates and insurance), you can also claim travel expenses to the property to collect rent, inspect the property or carry out maintenance. Keep in mind that only the costs associated with visiting the property are deductible. For example, Bettina's property is located in Broome, so her airfares to Broome and one

night's accommodation should be deductible. If she stayed a week to visit friends or have a holiday, though, the extra expenses would not be deductible.
- If you buy a new property you'll generally be given a depreciation report by a quantity surveyor. If you aren't, and the property was built after 1997, it might be worth paying for one. This may provide you with valuable depreciation deductions you may have otherwise missed out on.
- Repairs carried out on a property before leasing are generally considered to be initial repairs and are not immediately deductible (they instead add to the cost base of the property when you sell it).

For more information, visit Residex (<www.residex.com.au>), Australian Property Monitors (<www.apm.com.au>) and the Australian Bureau of Statistics (<www.abs.gov.au>).

Open house:
Bianca Dye's tuna salad

1 large tin of Italian canned tuna in oil
spinach leaves
baby vine tomatoes, halved
cucumber, chopped
squeeze of lemon
fetta cheese pieces

Mix all ingredients together and toss. I love tuna salad. Yum!

Chapter 5
Dinner for One

> *Financial fears? The great, mysterious, baffling world of tax.*
>
> —Jessica Adams, astrologer, author and citizen at large

When there's no-one else in the picture, how do single women manage? What's important for those 'dining alone' financially? The 2006 census data revealed that there were 1.74 million single households compared to 2.6 million 'couple' families—with a slight decline in this latter group since 2001. Singletons aren't evenly spread through the demographics: baby boomers are rocketing ahead in the single stakes, with the number of fiftysomething single people jumping by 793 000 in 2006. However, there's also been a surge in the number of people aged between 25 and 34 living solo. And single-parent families now account for 15.8 per cent of all families compared to 14.5 per cent in 2001.

There's no doubting that wealth can be created by a unit of one. However, there's a real divide between single women with no kids and single women who are mothers. The number-one worry of most single mothers is finding enough money for the kids and their needs (Superwoman research

2005). Still, while being newly single can be painful, it can be liberating too. You get to see what you're made of, and it can be empowering to revitalise your finances.

One of the primary assets all women have is their income. Yet despite the fact that lack of promotion will have a serious impact on their net worth, women tend to hold back when it comes to pushing the case for a pay hike. View your income as a good thing and treasure it! It's a key to your present and future wealth.

Women's participation rates in the workforce vary greatly, of course. Younger women without kids work at the same rate as men, but for mothers of the same age the rates plummet to 50 per cent (AMP.NATSEM *Income and Wealth Report* Issue 12, November 2005, p.14). However, older mothers are keener to get into work, and mothers over 45 have a higher participation rate in the workforce than younger working mothers—over 70 per cent!

Single in your twenties: takeaway time

Living at home and deferring rent in your twenties can really give you a financial edge. Liz Goodman is making the most of this time and proving that it can work well. At just 23, she's been investing in property for several years, is her own boss, and works and lives in her family's home. Liz is one of Nutrimetics' youngest executive managers and leads a team of 20-plus spa consultants from Menai, Sydney.

Liz took her first big financial step at just 19—buying an industrial unit with the encouragement of her mother and father:

> We paid about $45 000 for the units, and recently a similar one was on the market for $75 000 plus GST, so that gives you an idea of the increase in value.

Liz paid off that unit at the end of 2006, and she and her boyfriend Ryan aim to buy two more properties:

> Our plan is to buy some more positive cash flow properties; we're in the process of doing our research and due diligence right now. We'll buy the Residex report (a property report which shows the latest data on pricing trends), but we won't rush into anything yet. We'll just buy when the right deal comes along that suits our criteria. But once you've got the proper research, you should act.

One good thing about industrial property, says Liz, is that you don't have too many maintenance headaches with just walls and a concrete floor to look after. 'And it's important to start small too, because if something goes wrong, it's easier to recover!'

Katrina Pulbrook, an ANZ Financial Planner, gives her take on 'musts' for women in their twenties:

- Be careful that you don't listen to the wrong person. If you get advice from the family, make sure it's right for now. Grandparents may be too conservative to understand your life stage and want you to keep money in the bank rather than think about investing. On the other hand, it may be that your role model is into buying speculative investments. Again, be careful who you follow—what works for others may not be for you.

- Property may be something that your parents are keen on. While a mortgage is a form of enforced savings, you still need to plan your spending so you can meet your repayments. You need to be confident about the sustainability of your earning capacity.
- Some women may be driven to improve their overall outlook and income and therefore take on more risk, but you may be more comfortable with conservative approaches. So, listening to someone who's in a different financial place than you may not be appropriate. Risk tolerance counts for a lot: property involves debt, and so the risk attached to it is higher than for some other investments.
- You may need to think about combining your super if you've moved jobs, but if you only have a small amount, finding someone to advise on the fund switch may be tricky! Banks can be a good starting point if you have an existing account with one. If you've lost track of any super, search for it online via <www.findmysuper.com>.

The thirties: choosing from the career menu

There's a cost to exploring fresh career options, but in the long run it's probably worthwhile. Merryn Gruythuysen is wonderful example of someone who took a bold step in her late twenties and early thirties to reinvent her life and finances.

Merryn was a sales reporting analyst at a large communications company and earned $55 000 per annum. She cut back to part-time work and took on a HECS debt—

dropping $20 000 a year—so she could go back to university to study. Luckily, Merryn's friends and family were all for the change. She explains:

> I always wanted to be a nurse and I found corporate life just wasn't me! I still wonder if it was a bit of a whirlwind decision, but Mum and Dad were really great about it and helped me out. My friends were also very encouraging. It helped, because studying at home was a big change from going to work.

Now 31 and finished her three-year degree, Merryn is a registered nurse at one of Sydney's leading hospitals, and is looking to specialise in gastroenterology nursing.

> As a nurse, you start on $21 per hour, but what you take home depends on the shift. In my first year I earned $41 000 [base pay]. Of course, you can earn more doing afternoon and weekend shifts and night shifts. I do a lot of weekends. If you progress quickly through the ranks, you can earn good money quickly.

So how has Merryn made the financial adjustment to her new lifestyle? Here's what she's done:

- She uses a budget and has made cuts by taking her lunch to work and reducing takeout food, and it's made a big difference in her savings.
- She's continued to rent the same apartment and shares the rent and costs with a friend.
- She chooses not to have a car and all its associated costs, as she lives close to work and good public transport.

- She's cut her debts, including HECS, and cleared her $3000 credit-card balance by switching to a six-month interest-free card and paying the card off in that time.
- Her short-term savings goal is $5000; she wants to have enough in three or four years to buy a house or shares.

> I'm enjoying what I'm doing, but sometimes it's a struggle. I'm happier in terms of my job but I do have to think about spending and that can be stressful. I think about going back to Queensland because that would be easier and the living expenses are a lot lower — maybe that will happen.

Lisa Faddy, co-founder of financial planners Majella Wealth Advisers, says she's often surprised by how responsible single women in their thirties are about their money.

> Usually, they prefer to buy a home or an investment property because that's what they know and it's a form of forced savings. A lot of the time we get clients who already have a home loan, and we suggest diversifying investments and being tax-effective.

She has this advice:
- Save as much as you can, because if you plan to have a child at some point your income will go down. Have a regular savings plan, and debit the money out while you have a really good income and less debt.
- Diversify your investments outside of residential property. Even commercial property or property syndicates may be worth considering, because in the

past decade rental yields on residential property haven't always been good, and capital growth has been limited in some cities and suburbs. There's also a huge cost to getting into property—agents' fees, stamp duty and transactions costs.

- Once children come into the picture, life insurance cover and income protection is really important in case you get sick or injured and can't work. You can get some life cover through your super fund, but this may not be enough if there's only one breadwinner.

Cooking abroad: Jessica Adams

Astrologer and author Jessica Adams is at the elite end of her profession. Her predictions appear in international magazines in the UK, the US and Australia, and her novels sell well across several countries. Jessica has also been instrumental in setting up the *Girls' Night In* anthology series, which has raised millions of dollars for War Child projects in Africa, the Balkans, Iraq and Afghanistan (see <www.girlsnightin.info> and <www.jessicaadams.com> for more information). An Aussie with both an EU and an Australian passport, she divides her year between the UK and Australia—and as a result, faces the intricacies of tax on her earnings as an expat.

> I pay tax in two countries, and frequently have to include Europe as well (my novels are translated into several languages), so the maths sends me into a coma. The rules, regulations and red tape are beyond me; I rely heavily on my accountant, Helen, to sort everything out. I should know more about how it all works!

Many freelancers such as entertainers, contractors and athletes run into difficulties with international tax systems when their residency status is unclear. They may even end up facing double taxation, in the case of capital gains tax on assets that don't have a connection with Australia. It's important to seek advice on expatriate tax issues prior to going abroad to establish what you need to prepare for and how you want to structure your affairs. If you plan to go abroad indefinitely, it may be wise to sever local ties financially as much as possible.

When it comes to saving, Jessica wishes that she 'knew of websites that could save me time and money on almost everything—from price comparisons on whitegoods, to simple-language finance explanations. They must exist, but I've never found any!' And if she had spare money to invest?

> I'd invest in my own start-up dotcom, Travel Goddess Guides! It's a travel website by women, for women, which also helps to promote the *Girls' Night In* series.

The forties: putting more on the plate

The forties are a time where relationships may unravel one way or another for many women. Most commentators mention that divorce can be the very worst financial scenario and leave it at that! But it's not all bad, say divorcees. There's a new dawn after every night.

ANZ's Katrina Pulbrook likens a financially dependent relationship to an A-frame house and recommends that partnered women retain their independence. She explains:

If you take the arm off an A-structure, it will fall to the ground. But the shape of an H-structure means there would still be two poles standing—it's independent, and if either of you walk away then the structure remains. You may not be married forever. But there are lots of things you can do [to help yourself], such as super splitting. If your partner has put family assets with debt into your name, partly for tax purposes, then you may want to explore alternatives to holding assets with personal liability, like an investment company or trust structure.

While divorce is common among people in their forties, working women are also at their highest earning capacity at this age. If you've fallen behind for whatever reason, retraining or re-skilling is a good option; a lot of women in this age group return to formal studies. Your career is an asset and you need to invest in it. But how does that work for your cash flow? Should you stay in your home or sell it to cover costs? Part-time study or distance education allows for part-time work, so you may be able to keep up your cash flow that way. Katrina Pulbrook also mentions that you can get tax discounts off any investment expenses to help with cash flow. If they're approved by the Tax Office, they can be filtered back through your PAYG salary so you don't have to wait for the end-of-year tax return. See <www.ato.gov.au> for details.

Usually, your forties are a good time to explore turning points and become more independent, as your children (if you have any) are older. Women who had children later, however, may still have kids at primary school and the accompanying restraints on their time and financial burdens on their shoulders. 'You never plan to be on your own as a mother', says one woman who's raising a young daughter on her own. 'And that's what makes it harder.'

Peggy Barker, co-founder of Barker Wealth Management, comments:

- Divorced women often end up with the children, the family home (or part of it) and, if they're lucky, some extra cash and maybe a share of the husband's superannuation. Whatever the outcome, it's important to seek financial planning advice before you take on any new financial commitments.
- Every situation is different, so don't just rush out to buy a house immediately.
- Family Tax Benefit Part A and B are no longer assessed on your income, so it's easier to qualify.
- Now is a good time to review your income, and skill up and improve your qualifications if you've been out of the workforce.

An empty place-setting: being widowed

A large number of women have to deal with the premature death of a partner. Jane Durham* was widowed 16 years ago at the age of 34. While she had a window of three months to resolve their joint finances before her husband passed away from melanoma, it was still a shock.

Her husband was an actuary, and even though he'd taken the primary role in money matters, he'd encouraged Jane

* Part of Jane Durham's story first appeared in 'Shoulda, Coulda, Woulda?' by Julianne Dowling, *Vive* magazine, June/July 2007, p. 99.

to pay the household bills and understand their financial responsibilities. What took Jane by surprise was that their joint accounts became unavailable for a period after his death, and she didn't have much money in her own name to fall back on. (By law, when a death occurs, all bank accounts and superannuation in that person's name are frozen until probate, when the beneficiaries are determined by the executor of the will.) It also took a while for the insurance monies to be paid.

> That time was a bit of a blur. I just managed; I had to.
>
> As a result, I'm much more careful about spending.

These days, Jane owns her own home with a very small mortgage, which she can draw down if necessary. She also manages her own share portfolio.

Peggy Barker of Barker Wealth Management points out that in the unhappy event of losing a partner, all the financial responsibilities will fall on the survivor. She strongly suggests that couples consider getting life insurance — a lump-sum payment could make life a lot easier on the money front! In her opinion, the most tax-effective way to do this is within superannuation, as the lump sum can then be paid out tax-free. (You can also choose to receive the payout as a tax-effective income stream, if you prefer.)

> Whatever your situation, it's important that you get some financial advice before you do anything, as there could possibly be additional benefits such as anti-detriment payments for which the deceased member of the fund may be eligible.

An anti-detriment payment is a refund of the contributions tax paid by the member, but not all funds allow them.

Tupicoffs' senior financial planner, Neil Kendall, says one of the main issues for new widows is to get the big picture on their finances. That means going through policy documents, bank accounts, super fund documents, trust deeds, information on other investments such as shares, and any other key financial information: 'Generally, you're on a treasure hunt to find everything, and it can take time.' Don't be surprised, either, if the trustee of the superannuation fund writes to the deceased's children to ask if they want some money:

> In some cases, they may write back and say, 'Yes!' And the benefit you were expecting from the super fund may not be all yours. Knowing that the right amount of money is going to the right person takes preparation during life—not after death!

*Neil's recipe for the newly widowed

- Understand what wealth and assets you have. Check who receives the life insurance payout, as there can be many options and you may find that the payment is larger than expected. In the interim, you may be worried about what will happen and feel like you have virtually nothing but the house. It's crucial to have some rainy day funds in your name to tide you over.
- A jointly owned house can pass automatically to the spouse, but superannuation doesn't.

There are very different tax treatments for passing money to children and a partner or parents. If they're not dependants, parents' and children's benefits may be unnecessarily taxed.
- Don't make irreversible decisions immediately: take time to find what life is like before you make investment plans. Putting money straight into super, for example, may block your access to that money for a long time and leave you struggling if you haven't taken your new lifestyle into account.
- Understand any fee arrangements you're entering into with advisers or products and be 100 per cent comfortable with them. If you're doubtful now about what you're getting for the money, it may be a bad sign. Neil says: 'I've yet to read a financial plan that fully and clearly discloses all the fees and incentives. You shouldn't feel railroaded into signing before you feel you have a grip on what it all costs and are happy with it!'

The fifties: sipping piña coladas or water?

Over the age of 45, many people want to work less or work differently. But what happens if you haven't planned for that transition? What if your goals are still a long way from being realised? How can you make it happen faster?

Statistically, there'll be more fiftysomethings in a decade than there are today. Right now, the trend is for a third of Australians to retire by their mid to late fifties; of those remaining, three-quarters say they want to retire before they're 65 (AMP.NATSEM *Income and Wealth Report* Issue 12, November 2005, pp. 20–21). Funding their retirement for the next two decades is a big challenge, as the principal source of income for those over 65 is still government benefits—though most people don't expect that to be the case (AMP.NATSEM *Income and Wealth Report* Issue 12, November 2005, p. 21)!

About 18 months ago, Rose Elliot Jones, 52, whom we met in chapter 4, had given up hope that she'd retire comfortably. She'd resigned herself to thinking that she'd have to apply for public housing or live with friends, and would go on the pension. She suddenly realised that if she wanted to borrow money, she only had another decade left to qualify for a loan—time was a-tickin'!

> That's when I started to save again. I was aimless before that. Now, I feel better. I might just get through [to retirement] with what I'm doing by saving more and working hard.

Rose says that not having enough money is 'a bit like your health—until it comes up you may not think about it'. She has $52 000 invested with an industry super fund and has started taking advantage of the government co-contribution, which matches her 150 per cent on voluntary super contributions. Living in-house as a carer has allowed her to save well over $30 000, and this has been placed into credit society bonds, though she's considering moving across into high-quality shares. Given that she has a second, part-time income, her savings target is $50 000.

> Hopefully, I'm getting back on track. I'm a good saver; I don't spend at all. I said I'd never have a property, but now I'm thinking maybe I could have one after all.

Being single, Rose has to satisfy a lender that she can pay off the loan before retirement and also that she can meet the repayments. Has she left it too late? Not according to Robert Cribb, Wizard Belmont branch principal, who says there's no real age limit for finance:

> Each scenario tends to be different. However, if someone has 5 per cent plus stamp duty costs and allows another 5 per cent to cover purchase costs, as long as the interest repayments can be serviced, this would look okay [to the financiers].

The key point is that you need a steady income, not just assets, to get a loan.

Taking stock

Longer term financial plans are also critical when reviewing investment strategies. For women in their fifties, Peggy Barker of Barker Wealth Management suggests this to-do list:

- Take stock of what you've got. This is a good time to build up your wealth, especially if you're still working and are an empty-nester. You have 10 years left in the workforce, so review all your plans.
- Find a financial planner and sort out the big picture.

- Super is key, so accumulate while you can. The government has changed the rules on super—whether you're an employee or self-employed, you can co-contribute and get 150 per cent.
- Downsizing your house may be on the agenda; realising some of the equity in your home and putting it into super could provide tax advantages. You can also still invest in a range of assets and get good returns.
- Most property is worth more than $150 000, so granting you a loan may be an issue for financiers if you have few working years left to repay it. Check it out sooner than later.

ANZ Financial Planning's Praveena Sharma says that if you've left saving for superannuation until your fifties, you may need to consider a Centrelink pension to supplement your income on retirement. From 20 September 2007, a single person can still own their own home plus up to $161 500 in assets and get a full pension of $13 803.40 yearly. It then starts falling off by $1.50 a fortnight for every $1000 over the assets test, and ends once you've reached the cut-off point (see chapter 7 for more).

> Be mindful that your assets include everything you own (furniture, motor vehicles, boats, caravans, investment property, etc.) except your principal residence. Centrelink assesses the value of your household contents on a garage-sale level; your motor vehicle is assessed at market value. Since motor

vehicles depreciate quickly, it's worth reviewing this annually.

Praveena adds that depriving yourself in order to get full pension is not the way to go:

> If a couple have over $500 000 in superannuation assets, they may decide to focus on investment strategies to make their money last. Converting to allocated pensions allows investors to draw a regular income while giving themselves the opportunity to invest in growth assets. Just because you're retiring, doesn't mean your money is! It should be working even harder for you. You could live a long time, if family longevity and health is good.

Regular reviewing and monitoring of investment strategies is also imperative for financial success, and this is where advisers can help, by keeping clients informed of the changes and opportunities. Praveena says: 'Gone are the days of set-and-forget strategies. Because women are living longer than men, we need to take more responsibility for our money.'

Now that you've made your way through the singles maze, you deserve Jessica Adams's delicious, idiot-proof seafood pizza (over the page).

Idiot-proof entertaining: Jessica Adams's gourmet seafood pizza

Two plain cheese pizza bases
mozzarella cheese
brie cheese
anchovies
green prawns, peeled
raw scallops
crème fraîche
salmon roe

Buy the two best plain cheese supermarket pizzas you can afford. Bake them according to the directions on the packet, but pull them out 15 minutes early and decorate with lots of mozzarella and brie, plus the odd anchovy. Put them back in the oven until all the cheese has melted.

Cook handfuls of prawns and scallops in olive oil in a frying pan on the lowest heat. Remove when just done.

Pull the cooked pizzas out, throw on the prawns and scallops, drizzle some crème fraîche over them and sprinkle on some salmon roe.

In winter, serve this hot; in summer, serve it cold. Offer lots of side plates of grapes, cut-up fruit, strawberries and various salads—you can buy these or make them yourself.

Chapter 6
Chief Cook and Bottle-washer?

> *What doesn't make you stronger kills you — you're master of your own demise/success.*
> —Monica Trapaga, retailer, performer and mother to six

It's no wonder money can be a bit of a blur in women's minds: many of us have got so much on our plates already—jobs, parents, pets, kids, extended family, school demands. And then there are the events that can really stuff things up—death, divorce, disability, disease...

Generally, women earn less, have lower net worth and less superannuation than men; they also generally wind up poorer after a divorce. When you factor in all the caring responsibilities we shoulder, you can see why! Life sometimes gets in the way of happiness and meeting your own needs. Instead of just cooking a gourmet dinner for yourself and your partner (if you have one), so to speak, you may well have to act as chief cook and bottle-washer for a crowd. Consider these numbers:

- Over 50 per cent of Australians aged between 30 and 44 years care for kids under 15; once the kids are over three, over half the mothers have jobs.

- Nearly half a million Australians are carers. Of those under retirement age, a third care for their partner, a third for disabled children and a third for parents.
- On average, carers aged 35 to 54 have lower incomes than those without responsibilities.
- Nine out of 10 Australians under 65 who care for frail, aged parents are women — yet more women are participating in the workforce.
- Paid services that can fill the gaps for carers can be expensive.

Source: AMP.NATSEM *Income and Wealth Report* Issue 13, May 2006, p.4, p.10, p.12, p.21.

Women are facing more burdens than just their own wealth management issues, and they carry a high emotional and financial cost. Let's take a look at some of the different responsibilities women face and what financial options you have in each situation.

Cooking for children

Women with children face a burning issue: what do you do with the children when you have to work? Unfortunately, Australia's rudimentary and expensive childcare system is of little help. There's not much joy to be had in paying out your precious after-tax dollars on day care, nannies who require superannuation and work cover, or an unreliable babysitter. You wonder if it's even worth working — and it may not be.

However, the May 2007 budget finally recognised that women do need a helping hand, and as a result, the means-tested Child Care Benefit was raised by 10 per cent above the index. The maximum rate of assistance has gone up as a result by 41¢ an hour to $3.37. The other change entitled families to receive their 30 per cent rebate for both 2005–06 and 2006–07 from shortly after 2007–08 began — it was something, but not nearly enough. The income thresholds on the family benefits have remained the same.

Liesl Capper has a degree in psychology and is the CEO of RelevanceNow, a mover in the technology world. She comments that child care remains a vexing issue for her. She has even had to resort to extreme options like funding her overseas-based parents to come to Australia for a holiday when she had business trips!

> With two kids, I found I couldn't rely on normal day care, because nobody would fetch my children in their [opening] hours. I needed a nanny just to go to board meetings. She was paid out of my after-tax income, which sometimes meant that she put more in her pocket than I did!
>
> It's probably one reason why women stay in smaller businesses; I believe there's enormous talent out there that we're missing out on [as a result]. There's a massive, growing balloon of fifty-something women who are going to be dependent on the government. So making home-related stuff tax-deductible would help not just on a personal level but a national one.

Women in the sandwich generation (the thirties to fifties) can find themselves in a difficult position. Because many are choosing to have children later in life, they're not as prepared to give up their working lives—nor can they afford to, often, if the money has to cover a number of people. Cathy* asks a common question:

> What, if anything, can I claim for on our childcare arrangements? I'm thinking about resuming work in my own business, but finding it hard to get child care for our four-month-old baby. The three-year-old is already in day care two days at week at $38 per day; the baby will only be accepted for one day a week for $48 daily. Working means an extra $500 a week in hand—$20 000 a year—but child care costs us $9600 yearly plus the petrol costs for all the driving. Is it worth it, given all the extra travelling and hassle?

Michelle Pearce of Face Chartered Accountants answers:

> Under the new tax changes, you can claim the Child Care Tax Rebate upfront in the new financial year, and that may relieve the cash-flow impact. The underlying question here is whether it's worth working! Someone earning $20 000 per annum is pocketing about $18 000 after tax under the new tax thresholds. Additionally, that person will receive a 30 per cent rebate on childcare costs. Maybe if Cathy's partner is on the top marginal tax rate, he could claim for the upfront childcare costs and get a 30 per cent tax deduction, plus the extra benefit at the top marginal rate—which is, say, $1600. So the after-tax childcare cost is more likely

* Surname withheld on request.

to be $8000. You will probably be $10 000 better off in net earnings—but you may still need to consider the non-financial aspects of both being income-earners.

Cooking for parents

In my forties, I used to ask my father for advice. Later, it turned around and he was asking me!
—*Carol, 53, businesswoman*

So you've finally got your financial act together. Maybe you're working, earning an income, in the process of educating your children or have finished educating them. You've managed to get your super organised and work out what you'll do when you retire. Then life throws you a curveball—what about your parents? In the words of clinical psychologist Dorothea Vallianos:

> Suddenly, they're old and frail. They may not have saved enough; they've possibly underestimated their financial needs for their third trimester of life. Unexpectedly, you now face the death or illness of one or both parents (not to mention step-parents). How do you cope financially, let alone emotionally?
>
> You're facing the choppy waters of looking after your parents—either on your own or with siblings—and often those parents don't want help or can't see that they need it, and don't want to be 'parented'. They might say, for example, 'There's nothing wrong with my memory/mobility/balance' or 'I'm perfectly fine living on my own, I've been doing it

for years and I don't need to go to a nursing home — or to be treated like a child, thanks very much!'

The trigger for a crisis of this kind is often the death of one parent or a change in their assets. A parent's death can result in a probate period during which joint investments are temporarily frozen. You may find that the remaining parent is less able to cope with household management; bills go unpaid or forgotten, and perhaps they don't spend much on food. Women live longer, too, and our funds for that 'long, golden summer' just may not stretch to cope with twenty-first-century longevity.

Money is one of the last taboos. It's harder to talk about than sex and much harder to discuss within the family due to power balances within relationships, fear of losing control, or fear of ageing and potential loss of independence. But it must be done!

One question in particular to discuss with your parents may be the suitability of their investments. For example, ANZ Financial Planner Aiyuty Soetanto points out that money in a low-yield bank account may be good in the short term for emergency and liquidity purposes, but in 10 years' time the value of that money will be lower because of inflation:

> So you won't be able to buy the same amount [with that money] as you can today. Investing in property and blue-chip shares can be a good protection against inflation even within a 'retired' investment portfolio.

Deciding what you'll invest in during your older years doesn't mean taking on high risk. The test is how you sleep at night; if the investment sounds too good to be true, then it probably is.

Setting the table: the costs of care

In the case of the illness of one parent, things can get tricky. As Dorothea says:

> What happens if the other parent is in denial? What assistance can you give, and how do you intervene? If you're in that sandwich situation where you're the principal carer, what happens when there are other siblings? What if they take control and you're not happy about it?

Not all the answers to these sorts of questions are palatable, financially possible or emotionally satisfying. Dorothea's advice is to be practical and prepared: acknowledge what can and can't be done, seek assistance and then delegate. She suggests the following:

- Check out advice regarding dementia and Alzheimer's, the available financial help, accommodation and how your home might need to be modified should you have to care for your parent/s in future. Think about it now, so it's not as scary during a crisis.
- Arrange to speak with your parents in advance and find out what they want before they hit a crisis point — it may help all of you feel more secure about future options. How this conversation goes will depend on the sort of relationship you have with your parents and whether they welcome your support or not.

- Involve all the relevant family members. When family discussions occur at times of crisis there's a lot of emotion involved, and that can sway decisions in less practical or realistic ways.
- Brainstorm all the options and possible solutions—for example, your parent/s staying in their own home, moving to a retirement village or hostel, or staying with you or one of your siblings. If they move in with you, do you then keep working or become a full-time carer?
- Weigh up the options against your values—financial and otherwise. Are you doing what you *should* (what your society or your culture expects) rather than what is financially viable, practical and aligned with your values? Your values (and helping family members to remember their own) can help you and your family sort through the mire of decisions.
- List the pros and cons of each option for each person involved in the decision-making process, do some research on the options, agree on an action, implement it and evaluate how it went.
- Get support and ask for help when you need it.
- Don't forget to look after your own health—it's hard to look after others and make sensible decisions if you're not functioning on all cylinders!

Praveena Sharma, an ANZ Financial Planner who specialises in retirement planning, says it's a common dilemma for one partner to need high-level care while the other wishes to remain in the family home. The financial impact of their choices also depends upon whether they're getting Centrelink or Department of Veterans' Affairs benefits. She says:

Where one party chooses to remain in the family home while the other needs care, things change financially. The house isn't assessed as part of the pension, but investments are, and the couple may still need money for the nursing bond—hostel bonds can range from $100 000 to $350 000, and the demand for spots is high. So what will they live on? Those who have no savings may need to look at options such as reverse mortgaging their home to come up with a lump sum. But if the property is in joint names and they don't have enduring power of attorney, they won't be able to decide upon such options.

Praveena urges people to plan ahead while they can. The thought of ageing might be depressing, but it's a process that we all go through. However, baby boomers are likely to experience it quite differently to their parents:

> It's a crucial area. We are living longer, and as more and more baby boomers retire without adequate funding for their life expectancy, the financial strain on welfare is only going to increase. The government needs to look at how this will be funded in future.
>
> Make sure you consider the opportunity cost of full-time care—the bond money doesn't earn a return, nor does it keep up with inflation. One of my clients, a self-funded retiree, has decided to look after her partner at home and hire a carer as needed rather than pay the exorbitant bond.
>
> If a person is suffering from chronic dementia, it's better to agree on a course of action in advance

and know that their wishes have been taken into account—that they weren't pushed into it as a last resort. But regardless of what's chosen, there are big financial and emotional consequences, and most retirees leave it to the last minute rather than planning for it.

At the time of writing, new asset taper rates have increased the cut-off limits for Centrelink pensions, so more people will be eligible. Self-funded retirees earning under $80 000 and single people earning under $50 000 are also eligible for the Seniors Health Card, which provides pharmaceutical benefits and a number of other discounts.

Menu options in retirement: reverse mortgaging

Releasing the equity in your home through a reverse mortgage (where a lender makes payments to you in return for some of the equity in your home) may be an attractive option for some retirees who are cash-poor but asset-rich. Whether it's a good course of action depends upon the value of the house. Be aware that reverse mortgaging can also have estate implications and unexpected costs.

Mortgage Choice broker Belinda Sugars, who has a background in banking and financial planning, points out that you don't have to provide proof of income when applying for a reverse mortgage. Lenders with reverse mortgage products will generally only lend a maximum of 30 per cent of the value of the property; the lender will also have the house periodically valued.

> Sometimes, people choose to pay down the loan at a later stage—they may want the children to have the home, for example. There are lots of reasons why; there are many reasons people take out reverse mortgaging in the first place. A couple may invest the loan money for a retirement income. Or parents may reverse mortgage between $20 000 and 30 000 and give their child the cash for a house deposit or to buy a business. That becomes a living inheritance, and some parents really like the idea, because they want to see their children benefit from the money while they're still around.

According to Belinda, when reverse mortgages first launched in Australia, they were virtually unregulated and exorbitantly priced. These days, she claims you can get a more competitive rate, and fees and charges are becoming more affordable.

> Generally, people come at a stage when they really want the finance. They probably know someone who's done it already, so while they do worry about the debt and their equity in the house, they've got more knowledge about the progress of things.

Be aware that sometimes the lender will insist on, say, a minimum loan of $20 000, even if you only want $10 000. Belinda comments, however, that 'the borrower shouldn't be compelled to take a higher amount if they don't want it'.

Reverse mortgage settlements are certainly on the rise, with a SEQUAL/Trowbridge Deloitte study showing growth of 60.6 per cent in 2006 to $520 million. Lump-sum advances made up 80 per cent of those loans, and 72 per cent of loans were made directly with lenders. The average age of borrowers remained at 74 years of age, but new borrowers were slightly younger at 72 years of age.

Some helpful questions to ask:
- How much do you need now compared with how much the loan will cost in future?
- How will reverse mortgaging impact on your pension? It may reduce your social security entitlements, so seek advice beforehand.
- Will you have enough money left for aged care if you reverse mortgage your home?
- How will your dependants be provided for? What will be the effect on the beneficiaries of your estate?
- Is your lender a member of the Senior Australians Equity Release Association of Lenders (SEQUAL)? SEQUAL members offer a 'no negative equity' guarantee.

Reverse mortgaging pluses

- A reverse mortgage can help finance the early, active part of your retirement. The debt is paid off when the house is sold, you die or, in some cases, when you go into nursing care permanently.
- For some women, a reverse mortgage may be the only way to raise cash. You don't have to make any regular interest repayments, and you can take the money either as a lump sum or as a periodical payment over time.

Reverse mortgaging minuses

- If it's not paid down regularly, the interest bill will be more expensive than for other forms of debt because of the compounding interest. There can also be more fees to pay, and fees may apply if you fix the interest rate then want to sell the house and pay the loan off. Remember, you may not have a choice—you may have to sell your home if your health takes a dive.
- Reverse mortgages carry the threat of negative equity—meaning that your loan can become worth more than your home. This could happen if property values fall, but it depends upon the loan terms. As mentioned earlier, some loans are guaranteed not to exceed the value of the property.
- Reverse mortgages have tax, estate and social security implications. Consider getting professional advice on these points.
- Consumer watchdog *Choice* released a report in early 2007 which surveyed 23 well-known loan providers, including some banks, and found that inadequate consumer protections were in place. When it conducted a shadow shopping exercise among 10 brokers, *Choice* also found that a poor level of information was provided to borrowers. If you're considering a reverse mortgage, it may be worth your while to buy the full report online at <www.choice.com.au>.

The cost of disabilities

Sometimes, women don't just have ageing parents to care for—chronic illness in the family or a dependant with disabilities may be thrown into the mix as well. Along with all the other effects, this can have a significant impact on their finances.

Lobbyist Meredith Ward has two sons aged 10 and 11, and the eldest experiences high-functioning autism (Asperger's disorder). There are 30 000 Australian children living with autism; a report by the Autism Early Intervention Outcomes Unit estimated the community costs (both direct and indirect) at $7 billion. Unfortunately, the bulk of those costs still falls on the shoulders of parents and fundraisers.

A single income is the norm for families dealing with autism. Meredith is a single parent as well and works two casual jobs as a contractor totalling 17 hours a week. (She also puts in many unpaid hours as a public affairs officer for Autism Victoria.) At the time of writing, single parents have to work 15 hours a week to be eligible for federal government support. Single-parent pensions are no longer available for families with school-age children unless they satisfy the work condition—and there is no exemption for parents with children with disabilities! Meredith's mortgage is $490 per fortnight, and because her cash flow is uneven, she's 'learning fast how to budget and "scheduling" the things the boys like to buy'.

> Most families with autistic children do the best they can to stay on top, but it's not easy. Our capacity to work is limited because we have to care for our

kids—and we live with higher stress levels than most. Many parents purchase private therapy and support, because the government doesn't provide enough. Or they pay (like I did) for child care just to get some respite.

Some parents re-mortgage their home to come up with the funds for care and investing in education—something especially important for children with autism. She comments, 'We invest in our children's future and forego a comfy or secure retirement—there's not much other option'.

Parents living with an autistic child may also have to spend much more on cleaning, laundry and other costs, because the child may break and spill things more frequently. Meredith says:

> Families of children with autistic spectrum disorders (ASD) would be among the most disadvantaged; research shows that more than any other parents of children with other disabilities, parents living with autism have a higher incidence of depression, anxiety and marriage breakdown.

She explains that the Department of Education in Victoria doesn't recognise Asperger's disorder as an intellectual disability, and so children with Asperger's are not generally given school funding for additional support:

> Funding for support in the classroom tends to come down to luck, with some schools having better skills at applying for support. Money is very tight, and the

additional pressure weighs heavily sometimes. I try not to dwell on it. I'm hoping my tax return will provide some breathing space and relief, but having to work as a contractor means the cash flow issues really put me at a disadvantage. Life isn't the wonderful world that I'd expected—but I do try to look for wonderful in *my* world.

Meredith is currently working on a state plan with the Victorian Government that looks at where the support gaps are for ASD families, and how community services can better fill them. The typical needs are for respite care and access to specialised intervention services, and parents with work commitments also need recreational services.

Dorothea Vallianos has these suggestions for carers:

Sharing the load is important. When you feel you have to cope on your own, you can feel incredibly overwhelmed, which decreases your problem-solving abilities and increases your stress levels. It can also make you more vulnerable to anxiety and depression. Reaching out and networking is not only important for parents, but also for the children—it gives them the opportunity to foster relationships with other children and other adults, thereby developing social skills, slowly. It's probably best for Meredith or any family with an ASD child to network with families in a similar situation, so that they can help each other.

The new Medicare initiative for psychological services means that mum and child could both get the

Medicare rebate for counselling, if they get a referral to a psychologist from their GP.

Cooking in the country

ANZ Regional Financial Planner Lynelle Bower describes women in farming families as 'mighty women'. Not only do they care for their family, they often work on or off the farm and provide emotional support for their partners in troubled times as well. The theme of a farming life in tough conditions, like flood or drought, is high debt and low cash flow, so many of these women are in a double bind when it comes to retirement funds — or indeed any form of savings!

Colleen Peffer, senior financial planner with Bridges, Wodonga, explains:

> Generally, farming families see the farm as everything. If they have surplus money they don't use it for super: it's used to keep the farm going, every last cent. There's no quick fix either, because the farm [as a whole] may not be easy to sell. Third- and fourth-generation farmers don't usually want to leave anyway. However, there's generally a market for the land and the water rights, so farming families may consider selling off some of the land. In the regional towns, small businesses can have a more positive story. But the drought still affects the cost of living for everyone.

She observes that country women nevertheless work hard to keep on top of their finances:

> Women in the country are very aware of the government superannuation co-contribution and keep up to date with developments. A lot of women have their own share portfolios—they don't want to be destitute in their old age.

Colleen adds that while drought-relief and rural-assistance packages are available from Centrelink, many farmers find them hard to get because of the level of paperwork required. However, Exceptional Circumstances grants of $5500 are offered in areas that have been adversely affected for three years or more, allowing local businesses and farmers to get professional and financial advice. (To be eligible, businesses need to be in Exceptional Circumstances–declared areas, gain 70 per cent of their income from primary production and employ up to 20 people. For more information visit <www.daff.gov.au/droughtassist> or call Centrelink's Drought Assistance Hotline on 13 23 16.)

One of the other complaints about drought relief is that if family members are forced to work off-farm to keep things going, that income may count against them when applying for financial support under the '70 per cent farm income' rule. Yet farmers claim that the wages earned driving trucks or buses or working in town are not enough to support the farms, let alone feed the family.

Michelle Pearce, director of Face Chartered Accountants, reveals that there may be a new option for farming families in search of relief:

> More farmers may have access to farm management deposit accounts. The non-primary production income

allowable [to be eligible for one] has increased from $50 000 to $65 000 per year, and the total amount that can be held in those accounts has risen from $300 000 to $400 000.

Farm deposit accounts were created under a federal government scheme to help farmers manage their cash flow. They're savings accounts in which pre-tax earnings can be deposited in good years to allow cash reserves to build up to cover the leaner times. Tax is paid on any withdrawals; you may want to get tax advice for your specific situation.

✳ Kate's farmhouse recipe

Kate Schwager runs online portal service Webteam Australia, which hosts websites for regional western New South Wales towns including Wee Waa, Narrabri, Moree, Cobar and Trangie, and for Hughenden and St George in Queensland. Kate is also part of a primary-producing company that share-farms a property near Wee Waa, is the publicity officer for Wincott—the network for Women in Cotton—and is president of the local Chamber of Commerce. She has this advice for country women managing through tough times:

- Pay cash if you can.
- Don't live above your means.
- Pay yourself a wage from the company.
- Pay personal tax as you go, so there's no huge personal tax bill at the end of a year or quarter.

- Don't run everything through the company; keep your personal expenses separate.

My view is to stay positive and dream of when it will be better. Talk to the bank and have ideas in reserve for when things [get difficult]. Talk to people; don't ignore those you owe money to, and try to pay a little to each creditor. Set yourself up a payment plan to pay it back, and don't give up! If you live in a country town, people admire you more for having a go and paying it back.

Protection from accidents

Amid all these different responsibilities—whether they be child care, ageing parents, family members with disabilities or tough times on the farm—it's easy to lose sight of your priorities and what's important. Sometimes, lack of action simply comes down to being time-poor and overburdened.

Considering your personal risks and how to protect yourself through insurance is one example. Women tend to be fans of self-funding rather than of taking out private health insurance and income-protection insurance, but you really need to ask yourself: is this such a good idea? Selling off your assets to pay hospital bills may not suit you when the time comes—and what if you don't have enough assets to sell?

Take Naomi Tamakuni's predicament. Naomi, a single working mother, had no home and contents insurance when a house fire destroyed most of her furniture and possessions, not to mention her two children's Christmas presents. Although the fire started in a neighbouring house, the neighbours' insurance will only cover them — not Naomi. Unfortunately, she'd got two online quotes for insurance off the web just before Christmas, but had been too busy to lodge an application.

> One thing that the house fire made me realise was that I'd given away too much of myself to too many other things, and hadn't focused on what was really important to me: the children and the home. I thought I could survive anything, so really, this should be fine. But I do feel gutted.

Fortunately, with the support of the local newspaper, the community came to Naomi's aid, providing donations of furniture and food, and her friends rallied around the family to offer both practical and emotional support. 'It just goes to show that you're not entirely alone. I'd never have thought this would happen, but I'm so surprised by what people have done for us.'

Naomi's case isn't unusual. A large proportion of householders either don't have home and contents insurance or are underinsured — a fact which is evident after every large-scale natural disaster. ANZ Financial Planner Carla Chambers says insurance is often seen as dispensable:

> We're blasé — it's not until things happen closer to home that we look more carefully at our own needs. [Even if you think you can't afford it, it's] better to have a little bit of insurance than nothing: structuring your insurance to bring your premium down may be one option.

She adds that income-protection insurance can also be crucial—you may not have much of a future without an income!

✳ *An insurance recipe*

Ian Chamberlain, business development manager of Insuranet, has these suggestions:

- If you're an owner/occupier, it may be better to combine your home and contents policies to ensure there's no dispute between insurers about what's contents and what's structure (like fitted dishwashers or air conditioning) in the case of a fire. This should also mean a lower premium, as administration costs are reduced.
- If you have a strata title unit, the banks will most likely insist on mortgagee's interest insurance. However, contents will be your primary insurance because the body corporate will cover the insurance on the common areas (stairwells, lobby and gardens) and any permanent fixtures that are seen as part of the building. Areas not covered by the body corporate insurance include the apartment interior and maybe the balcony.
- Check your insurance document for exclusions. For example, typically most insurers won't pay for flood run-offs under standard cover, so if you're in a flood-prone area, you may have to seek extra cover—if you can get it. Damage to a property that's been left unoccupied for over 60 days may also not be covered.

- Cheap policies aren't the best: you get what you pay for. House and contents policies come in two types: defined events and accidental damage. An accidental damage policy covers a wider range of incidents and losses than a defined events policy, but has a bigger premium.
- Renters must take responsibility for their own property and take out contents insurance to cover it. A tenant can't call on their landlord's policy if their own belongings are damaged.

Recipe for a sandwich-generation life: Monica Trapaga

Singer, TV presenter, retailer and landlord Monica Trapaga may not spring to mind as a typical 'sandwich-generation gal', but if you diarised a day in her life, you can see that she definitely fits the criteria. Monica got her first big break as a musician with Monica and the Moochers, and later moved into TV as a presenter on *Better Homes and Gardens* and *Play School*. These days, she has two companies—one covering her entertainment interests and the other for her two vintage homewares stores, Reclaim by Monica Trapaga, in Glebe and Summer Hill.

Her life may seem busy and glamorous, but she's had her share of heartaches and headaches. When her partner was diagnosed with a chronic illness, she continued working and looking after her own children through their school years, as well as four stepchildren.

> My mother lives on the Central Coast. I don't drive, which is a bit tricky, so I don't get enough time to spend time with her … I've inherited a lot of kids, and my priorities are with them.

She's also faced some very taxing times in business. Her initial retail venture, a pet shop, was problematic. There were lots of financial dramas and she had to contend with caring for some not-so-robust pets as well! She admits:

> I tend to be a person who's immediate and just thinks about getting through the next year. The pet shop disaster was a big learning curve. I had to go into overdraft to pay people, but I'd rather maintain my reputation. It has made me tougher about recovering money. I want to pay for my life and put my kids through private school.

Her home-decorator shops sell vintage homewares largely reclaimed by Monica. She also does much of the maintenance on the two shops and her property, and despite her ability to make good money, she's not a big spender. In fact, money isn't that important to her: experiences are. When her brother asked her to go to Spain with him to meet the family and celebrate her fortieth birthday, she decided that she and the kids would raise the money for the trip by selling stuff at the markets together.

> Spending time together and being a hands-on parent is really important. My kids know I work hard, but anything I have I'm happy to share. So they can have lovely things. But you have to limit it.

Women have to cope and not talk about money, but men love to talk about it, because they don't have anything near as much on their plate to juggle. They also love to show it off!

Monica's tips

- Money is the thing that I need enough of to do what I want and get to where I want. I always think, 'Have I got enough for a mortgage, to pay for private school fees and to cover expensive dentistry?' I do love the chance to travel too.
- Go with what you love and don't lose focus!
- Work isn't everything. Spend time with the kids; nobody has on their epitaph that they spent too much time with the kids.
- Be financially independent. It's the old Virginia Woolf thing; it gives you strength as a person.

Family favourite: Monica Trapaga's pasta salad

500g spiral pasta (or similar)
1 cup fresh basil leaves
1½ cups bocconcini cheese
1 punnet cherry tomatoes
1 punnet yellow pear tomatoes
1 cup grated Parmesan cheese

Dressing
½ cup olive oil
1 clove garlic, crushed
juice of 1 lemon
freshly ground black pepper and salt to taste

Cook the pasta until al dente and let cool. Tear up the basil leaves, chop the bocconcini and set both aside.

Make the dressing in a large bowl: pour in two-thirds of the olive oil, crush in the garlic, squeeze in the lemon juice, add the pepper and salt, and whisk. Add the tomatoes and bocconcini to the bowl and toss to coat with the dressing. Then add the basil and toss; the pasta and toss; then the Parmesan and toss again. Drizzle the last bit of the olive oil over the top and give one final toss.

You can also add ingredients such as toasted pine nuts, capers, olives or other fresh herbs if you like. This is great with crusty bread. Enjoy!

Chapter 7
The Super Souffle

> Actually, I don't have much super, because my father told me to invest in real estate instead.
> —Jane Rutter, flautist, author and performer

Let's face it: superannuation is a bit like the proverbial souffle—you hang around worrying how it's going to turn out and if it will ever rise. Problem is, most people don't like putting the money away, and often we don't want to think about it until it's almost too late.

Super is nothing more than enforced saving—a compulsory 9 per cent of your income under the grandly termed 'superannuation guarantee' that began in 1992–93. The guarantee applies to employees who are Australian residents, earn more than $450 a month, and are between 18 and 70 years of age. Domestic workers who are employed less than 30 hours and the self-employed are generally exempt.

Because compulsory super is a relatively new thing, the average worker will still receive a third of their retirement income from the pension. (*True state of super revealed for the first time*, AMP media release, 25 July 2007, on *The AMP Superannuation Adequacy Report*.) And even the long-overdue changes to superannuation laws in 2006 and 2007 may not make a significant difference to people with low super balances—or to younger people, who may have heavy home mortgages. However, for those with higher balances, super is now a much sexier option: there's a tax-free handout on retirement, in particular for baby boomers and self-managed super funds.

Figures published in 2007 show that each boomer has, on average, $381 000 net wealth, and most of that lies in the family home—42 per cent of people fall into this category. Super comes second when talking about net wealth, at 17 per cent (AMP.NATSEM *Income and Wealth Report* Issue 16, March 2007, p. 1).

Women, however, fall short on super projections, and are likely to have an average balance of just $77 000 by 2019, compared with men's average of $121 000 (Investment and Financial Services Association report, *Money Matters for Women 2004*). The Association of Superannuation Funds of Australia (ASFA) calculates that payout balances on retirement in 2006 are likely to be $45 000 for women and $130 000 for men, which is very low if you're planning to use it for income in retirement! Furthermore, 90 per cent of women have low amounts in super funds. AMP and Access Economics calculate that the average level for actively contributing women in their forties at December 2006 was under $40 000. For those in their fifties, it ranges between $42 000 and about $53 000 (*The AMP Superannuation Adequacy Index Report 2007*).

Generally, women understand that super is an essential ingredient for their future, even if it's a big yawn in the interim. As you get older, it comes up more on your radar. Jenny, 53, divorced with one grown-up child and working as an administrator, is in a pretty good position:

> I've been to a lot of seminars and consultants to try and understand my super better. I'm in two versions of funds — the defined benefits fund through State Super and an open fund. In the government one, the longer you stay, the better the outcome, and I've actually maxed out my contributions with this fund. I started contributing in 1991 and you can only go to a certain number of points. I'm working at a university now, so I've got another fund that I can salary sacrifice into. I feel okay about the balances.

Not so for Julie — at 50, she's in her second marriage and has worked for most of her life, yet still faces a super shortfall:

> When I worked for the public service while doing university, the Commonwealth Government matched contributions dollar for dollar. I had 10 per cent going into super and it was rolled into a tax-free bond, but my first husband got it in the divorce settlement. My first husband and I lived off my income while he maxed up his super. Then, I worked for someone for almost eight years, and they went bankrupt and hadn't paid the super for the employees. So I have a huge gap, and I'm funding it through my annual bonus and using a re-contribution strategy for salary sacrificing. Hopefully, that will bump me up.

ANZ Financial Planner Aiyuty Soetanto adds:

> Many younger people still don't like to think about it, but superannuation isn't an investment—it's a structure, and one that may have many tax benefits. When you're young and have a family, it may not be on your wish list. But it's good to have super on your wish list. If you pay off the house and have no super or any other investments, how will you feel? Owning your own house isn't diversified. And if you decide to borrow again and go back into debt, where does that leave you in your old age?

Often insurance is the backstop for those facing debts close to retirement. Insurance within super remains popular because of the cost benefit, but there are still drawbacks, Aiyuty says:

> Depending upon your family situation, it can be cost-effective to have life insurance within super as long as you have a nominated beneficiary who is a spouse or classified as a dependant. But this may not work so well for an older child or a sibling, because they pay tax on a slightly higher level, at 16.5 per cent—it's a bit unfair on people without dependants. For younger people, life and total and permanent disability insurance may not work within your super fund, because they can't get the money out until age 55 or over. At the end of the day, what's the purpose of insurance? If it's to help pay off debt liability, then you may want to consider the merits of keeping it outside of super.

Quick and easy souffle fixes

Not everyone needs or can afford professional advice each year, and the good thing about super is that there are little things you can do yourself to improve your situation. There are no secrets to making your souffle rise: all the information you need is on websites and in the media.

For example, dependent women and those on lower incomes can benefit from the government co-contribution—something that can really add up over the years. Basically, if you earn between $28 000 and $58 000 a year, you'll qualify for some government matching of any voluntary super contributions you make. If you earn under $28 000 a year, you'll receive $1500, provided you match it with $1000.

And even simple things like not giving your tax file number to your super fund can cost you. Under the new laws, if you don't, you'll pay an extra 31.5 per cent tax on employer contributions!

Here are some other small improvements to consider:

- Websites like <www.rainmaker.com.au> and <www.superannuation.asn.au> allow you to compare super fund features, fees and performances. They also give you some ideas of where you can place your money if your souffle isn't rising at your current fund!
- Make sure you understand the investment options within your super fund and have chosen the one that's right for you. There are usually a handful of options, termed something like 'growth', 'balanced', 'capital stable' and 'capital guaranteed'. Growth funds invest in growth

investments (Australian or international shares and property, through property trusts or direct investment) and are designed to provide a greater return over the long term. A typical balanced fund will hold 50 per cent or more of its assets in growth investments, with the balance in fixed interest, bonds and cash. Capital-stable funds hold more fixed interest (usually a minimum of 60 per cent), with the remainder in shares. Although these funds are vulnerable to interest-rate rises, the manager aims to minimise fluctuations. With capital-guaranteed funds, the amount invested or the income stream is guaranteed. If you're comfortable with the higher risk, opting for a bigger proportion of 'growth' investments may boost your super, as these have more potential for making higher returns in the long term.

- Consolidate your super accounts so you don't lose too much to fees. If you have little bits of super in different funds, this is a must. A recent study by *Choice* says that we waste $1 billion a year in fees! Almost 1.8 million super fund accounts were established in 2006, and only 20 per cent were consolidated. According to *Choice*, having even two funds made a significant impact on performance because of the fees.
- Keep contributing and think about salary sacrificing, especially if you get a pay rise or are self-employed.
- Keep up-to-date with changes to superannuation law if you're approaching retirement age. You're allowed to own a lot more assets than before to qualify for part or full pensions and/or the Seniors Card. In particular, keep up with the news around Federal Budget

time—the media is a free and fantastic information source on the never-ending changes and new scenarios.

Following the recipe definitely makes for a better meal!

That said, while there are lots of things you can do yourself, talking to a financial planner and getting the right advice at the right time can make a big difference to your payout at retirement. Many people choose a planner associated with their bank or someone recommended by friends or family. Some industry and public super funds also offer financial advice to members through their customer service centre. If you prefer, you can find lists of qualified planners in your region through the Financial Planning Association (<www.fpa.asn.au>) or through Select Adviser (<www.selectadviser.com.au>).

Changes to super law: simpler souffles?

After the 2007 introduction of the *Simplified Superannuation* initiative, many people thought (understandably) that super would be simpler and there would be less need for financial advice. That's not necessarily the case. The new rules have far-reaching implications—and worryingly, many retirees and semi-retirees don't know what the changes actually mean for them. According to a 2007 Mercer Human Resource Consulting study, 70 per cent of respondents could not articulate any of the Simpler Super changes (*Simpler Super Dividing Baby Boomers, Mercer Survey Finds*, media release, 4 May 2007, <www.mercersolutions.com.au>).

You get an idea of how disturbing this is when you consider the areas affected by the May 2006 Budget:

- superannuation benefits
- transition to retirement
- reasonable benefit limits (RBLs)
- age-based deduction limits
- superannuation rules for the self-employed
- undeducted contributions
- social security
- existing pensions
- super splitting.

And there were yet more super changes in May 2007, including:
- Since July 2007, divorce and capital gains tax relief on super transfers has meant a spouse can transfer assets from a small super fund to another complying fund without triggering capital gains tax.
- There was an increase in the super co-contribution. If you made an eligible contribution in 2005–06, then you were allowed a one-off co-contribution that doubled the amount already paid to you.
- Changes to the income assessment for the senior Australians tax offset mean you can now earn slightly more without paying tax.

Over the next few pages, we'll go through the 2006 and 2007 changes very briefly—if you need further details on anything, be sure to speak to a financial adviser and/or visit <www.simplersuper.treasury.gov.au>.

Changes to superannuation benefits

In the May 2006 Budget, there were major changes to the treatment of superannuation benefits, effective on 1 July 2007.

Here are the key points:
- Benefits paid from a superannuation fund after age 60 (whether that's a lump sum or you're drawing a pension) are no longer taxed.
- Tax is still payable on benefits paid to anyone under 60, but under more simplified rules.
- RBLs have been abolished.
- Compulsory cashing rules were abolished, which means you're no longer forced to retire and take super at 65 if you don't satisfy the work test.
- Retirement income stream/pension rules work in a simpler way.

In the past, many people were afraid of pushing too much of their wealth into super because the government often changed the rules. However, since these latest changes there seems to be a new mood. It's often better for retirees to hold assets as part of their super now because of the tax concessions.

Transition to retirement

Under the transition to retirement strategy, salary-sacrifice contributions to super can be made even if you're already drawing income from an allocated pension. This will potentially save a large amount of tax, especially for people at preservation age and over. If you're under 60, you can draw down up to 10 per cent of the fund balance in any one year as a pension after 1 July 2007.

No more reasonable benefit limits

Before 1 July 2007, you could only accumulate up to $1.3 million in superannuation if you wanted to be taxed at the special rate of 15 per cent (the 'concessional' rate). The good news is that, now, there's no limit on how much is tax-exempt or concessionally taxed.

No more age-related restrictions on contributions*

From 1 July 2007, the new single-person limit is $50000 per annum, with exceptions for those aged between 50 and 69 until 2012. After that, they fall in line with the universal limit, and penalties apply if you exceed it. Effectively, the government wants you to put more in when you're younger.

Individuals also now have five extra years—to age 75—to arrange deductible contributions to super, whether that's salary sacrifice or personal contributions.

Contributions by the self-employed are deductible*

If you're a sole trader or own a business, from 1 July 2007 you receive a full deduction for your super contributions, just as employees do for contributions made on their behalf.

You're also eligible for the government co-contribution scheme; a small personal contribution is required to qualify. Claiming the co-contribution can be a good way of funding your insurance premiums within your super fund or increasing your existing levels of cover.

New limits to undeducted contributions

From 2007–08, undeducted contributions are limited to $150000 per year.

* Additional material sourced from Genesis Financial Partners budget bulletin March 2007.

Social security changes

Changes to social security mean that the assets test will be more generous and you may qualify for a part pension or additional pension. Two of the major changes from 20 September 2007 were:

- A homeowner couple is allowed more assets under the pension asset test.
- All your complying income streams (pensions) are now counted under the asset test, where previously only 50 per cent was counted.

The new social security asset limits

Family situation	Asset limit for full pension	Asset limit for part pension
Single		
Homeowner	Up to $166 750	Under $529 250
Non-homeowner	Up to $278 750	Under $650 250
Couple		
Homeowner	Up to $236 500	Under $839 500
Non-homeowner	Up to $375 500	Under $960 500

Source: Centrelink Financial Information Service, <www.centrelink.gov.au>.

There haven't been any changes to the treatment of transfers from overseas superannuation funds, which are taxed in Australia. Remember that most overseas super transfers are classed as undeducted ('non-concessional') contributions, so they do count toward the new super contributions limits.*

*Existing pensions**

In the past, pensions were a bit confusing, ANZ Financial Planner Aiyuty Soetanto points out—there were so many different pensions and related dates to keep up with! Fortunately, with the 1 July 2007 changes, things have been simplified. One of the major changes is that there is no maximum pension payable. The minimum pension is 4 per cent of the total value of your superannuation.

Between the ages of 55 and 60, you may experience a variation in tax due to changes on the pre-1983 super component, which is now tax-free. Your pension amounts will also be affected by changes to the life expectancy tables. If you're over 60 and receive a pension, all your pension payments and benefits will be tax-free anyway, and a trigger event will only have practical effects if you die and benefits are paid to non-dependants. The trigger events are:

- turning 60
- partial or full commutation of your existing pension (that is, you take some or all of it as a lump sum)
- your death.*

Aiyuty adds, 'If you have a few [separate] allocated pension funds, you may want to consider combining them, given that there are no RBLs anymore'.

Eleven super questions

Superannuation can throw up a big menu of questions. In this section, we look at 11 of the most common.

* Additional material sourced from Genesis Financial Partners budget bulletin March 2007.

1. I'm thinking of changing my fund. What do I do?

This depends upon the type of fund you're in. Most people are in an accumulation fund, and under the super choice rules, you can only change your fund once a year. Defined benefits funds are closed to the public—they tend to be for public servants and favour those who have been in them for a long time. You can also run your own super fund with other trustees if you have the nous: generally, you'll need over $150 000 in super. If you, as a trustee, decide to move out of a self-managed super fund (SMSF), then your benefit can be transferred to a complying super fund. The remaining trustees must ensure that the fund still meets the definition of an SMSF. This may mean appointing a replacement trustee or a corporate trustee. The fund could also be wound up (ATO booklet *DIY Super—It's Your Money... But Not Yet!*, July 2004).

If you change jobs and you belong to an open fund, it's a good time to review how your fund compares with others. Do your research on the web—you'll find some helpful sites are listed earlier in this chapter—and make an appointment with an adviser if you feel you need to. According to the Australian Securities & Investments Commission's Fido website (<www.fido.asic.gov.au>), there are four good reasons to switch your super fund:

1. if your fund isn't available through your new employer
2. if you need to consolidate several super accounts to cut costs and paperwork
3. if you find other funds have lower costs or better features that would suit you more
4. if your current fund's investments have performed poorly over five years compared with similar funds.

It's *not* a good idea to change funds as a knee-jerk reaction to a short-term negative return or in order to jump onto the bandwagon of the year's best performer. Long-term returns are what matter with super, generally speaking, and the top performer may well be a different fund next year!

2. When should I start worrying about super?

If you're employed, your employer will make the compulsory super contribution for you—but remember the co-contribution. The longer your money is in a fund, the more the effects of compounding will work for you, so the earlier you can bump up contributions, the better the result.

3. How do I decide between the options in my fund?

The answer to this is to understand your attitude to risk and align your expected returns accordingly, says ANZ Financial Planner Praveena Sharma. As we mentioned earlier, you'll generally be offered four or five different streams with names like 'growth', 'balanced', 'capital stable' and 'capital guaranteed'. These offer different levels of risk—'growth' carrying the highest risk and 'capital guaranteed' the lowest—and their expected returns are accordingly higher or lower. The exact definition of each stream, what it invests in and in what proportions (called the 'asset allocation'), varies between funds. Praveena also points out:

> What you need to really think about is the length of time that you're investing for. People usually retire between the ages of 55 and 65 but live a lot longer, so the money has to last. Upon retirement, they may

switch to more stable investments, but the money will still be invested for, say, 20 or 30 years more!

4. How do I consolidate my superannuation accounts?

Do you know where your super is? There is a number of websites, including <www.ato.gov.au/super>, that can help you find accounts you may have lost track of. You definitely don't want to have as many super funds as you have spices in your pantry! But don't forget the exit and entry fees—there can be a short-term cost to rolling all your accounts into one.

5. How much super do I need to retire?

The Australian National University is researching this question, because spending patterns can be uneven post-retirement. For a couple retiring at 60, $50 000 per year is considered by most advisers to provide a comfortable lifestyle, and you'll need $600 000 in super to generate it. However, ASFA considers a modest couple's requirements to be just $26 154 a year! It makes sense to look instead at how much you spend now, and then think about how that might change at 55 or 65 years of age, to get an idea of what you might need. According to ANZ Financial Planner Carla Chambers, 'Generally, this exercise gives people a bit of a wake-up call! Some people can spend as much post-retirement as they do pre-retirement. Travel is a really big thing with the retired group too'.

Once you've settled on an annual income figure, use an online super calculators to work out how much you need to save to get it, and what monthly and yearly super contributions you'll need to make. (A series of calculators are available at <www.anz.com.au>; AMP offers a free CD called 'Thinking ahead' and a super simulator on its website, <www.amp.com.au>.)

6. When can I retire? What if I change my mind and go back to work?

You're free to retire at any age—the question is, what do you plan to live on? If you need your super to survive in retirement, then the earliest age you can retire is 'preservation age'. Preservation age is the age at which you can access your benefits in the super fund—it generally rises from 55 years if you were born before July 1960 and stops at 60 years if you were born after June 1964. But if you want to go back to work, you can, provided you meet the work tests for your age range. That means you can start a new super fund.

7. When can I get my super?

You can start accessing your super from your preservation age. How it's taxed, though, depends on what money is in the fund—this is where advice comes in handy. If you've made after-tax contributions, you can withdraw the money out of your super fund tax-free. At the time of writing, you can withdraw up to $135 590 tax-free from employer contributions, in many cases. If you draw out an allocated pension, you can get about $31 000 a year tax-free.

8. What's better: a lump sum or a pension?

It depends, says Carly O'Keefe, Adviser Solutions Marketing Manager for Tower Australia:

If you're tempted to take your money as a lump sum, you need to consider whether you're paying tax. Pensions can be tax-free if structured the right way. When you withdraw the money, you'll be paying tax on any investment earnings if you reinvest it—again, if you invest a pension, the earnings can be tax-free.

Aiyuty Soetanto, of ANZ Financial Planning, also warns:

> Do you want the funds to last your lifetime? A lump sum may not! And once you take money out of super, you may not be able to put it back, so take care.

9. What can I do if I don't have enough to retire on?

If you want to, you can just keep working—you don't have to withdraw your super at any particular age. If that doesn't sound like fun, Carly O'Keefe explains some other options:

> This is where your home is your helping hand. You can consider downsizing and moving the surplus profit across to super. For those who don't want to do that, there's reverse mortgaging. This allows older people to borrow money by mortgaging their home, without having to pay back either the amount borrowed or the interest due until they leave the home or die. There are real risks associated with reverse mortgages, however, and you need to make sure that it's a suitable solution for you. Seek qualified financial advice—and not just from a mortgage broker.
>
> Don't forget, either, that you may be eligible for the age pension, for rent assistance if you rent, and

you may also receive a pensioner concession card. The benefits of the Seniors Card varies from state to state, but it generally offers discounts on medicines through the Pharmaceutical Benefits Scheme; savings on property and water rates; savings on energy bills; a telephone allowance; and discounts on car rego and public transport. The asset tests determine if you qualify for full or part pension or the card. Something is better than nothing!

10. What happens if I outlive my retirement money?

It's good that you're asking this question: most women don't believe that they'll live to 85 or 90 years of age, ANZ's Carla Chambers says. If you run out of money, you have basically the same options given in question 9 — the age pension, selling off your home or reverse mortgaging (which was discussed in chapter 6). In relation to reverse mortgaging, Carla adds:

> Twenty years ago, I came across reverse mortgaging in the UK; now it's here. Sure, the interest is substantial because of the compounding, but if you want to stay in your house and you're not concerned about the estate planning consequences, then this can be an option to consider. Some retirees prefer to enjoy [their retirement] rather than leave money to their children. Also, it's not unusual for the children to be in a stronger financial position than their parents. A common view is that the client has worked hard for a very long time and they deserve to reap the rewards.

11. What's super splitting?

Superannuation splitting is dividing superannuation contributions with your spouse (married or de facto). This can help ensure that both partners have equal super balances, especially where one doesn't work or earns a low income. You can split employer contributions, and you could previously also split personal contributions. However, there are new rules. You can split 85 per cent of taxed contributions made after 6 April 2007 (like the employer compulsory contributions and salary-sacrifice contributions). If the contributions were made before 6 April 2007, you can split 100 per cent of the untaxed contributions (your personal contributions, spouse contributions, and so on).

Anne-Marie Esler, Technical Research Manager for Centric Wealth, comments:

> When super splitting was first introduced, there were many benefits to equalising superannuation balances between spouses. These were mostly derived from having access to two reasonable benefit limits and two tax-free thresholds. With the changes to superannuation, including the abolition of RBLs and tax-free super for the over-60s, super splitting has become a less effective strategy.

Praveena Sharma, ANZ Financial Planner, adds:

> With the abolition of RBLs, this strategy may be suited to those who plan to retire between the ages 55 and 60 to maximise the low-rate cap amount, which

is tax-free. If a client on a high salary has a significant amount in super and is able to salary sacrifice, then they could split 85 per cent of those contributions... Not only would this build the spouse's super, but they can use two tax-free limits. But if they retire after age 60 then they pay no tax, so there may be no need for this strategy, except hedging against future changes to super legislation.

Be mindful, she also says, that contributions cannot be split if the receiving spouse at the time of splitting satisfies a 'condition of release' (that is, the spouse can access the funds) — to ensure that the funds aren't immediately available.

Sources: ANZ Financial Planning, AMP, Centric Wealth, Tower Australia.

Some curly super-souffle questions

Women often have particular twists and turns with their super as a result of things like divorce, relocation and death. It can be quite complex. Below, we've given just a few typical issues experienced by women in their thirties, forties and fifties, with answers from experts.

Q. My family of four moved to Sydney from the UK five years ago, and we've left money in a pension fund there. How do I bring the money to Australia?

Louise Biti, Head of Technical Services, Asteron, answers:

Since late 2007, you've needed to be mindful of the super contribution limits for your age in Australia and ensure that you don't exceed them. How much money you can bring across from the UK will also be determined by the UK fund rules. If the fund allows a partial withdrawal (and not all do), you can take the amount under the Australian contribution limit and do it in a couple of stages. If it doesn't allow that, then you'll have to bring all the money across, but that may incur penalty tax.

So the question is: do you just leave it over there and take it as a foreign pension? Or bring it here and pay some penalty tax? Or if you're lucky, bring some of it here and leave some of it there?

You need to check your options and look at your circumstances. If you've been here for six months or more, you also need to look at the tax implications on the transfer amount. Decide whether it's better to have the fund pay the tax or pay it yourself—and whether you have that option!

You can choose to leave the money in the UK and access it as a pension on retirement. Keep in mind, though, that since the rules changed on 1 July 2007, Australian pensions are tax-free while the UK pensions are taxable. So if you're retiring now, the money may be better off here.

In the 2007–08 financial year, the maximum deductible contribution in Australia is $150 000—although you can use the three-year limit. Say you had a super balance of $450 000 in the UK: you could transfer half of it this year and half next year, if you're under 65, but in the next two years you couldn't contribute anything more. If your balance was $650 000, then you can transfer it all this year, but the amount above $450 000 will have a 40 per cent penalty. Some funds require you to commute (transfer) 100 per cent; some allow a partial commutation. So you have to check.

If you transfer money over here, there are two parts to the transfer. Most will fall into the undeducted contribution category. But if you've been a resident for more than six months, then the growth in the fund since you've been a resident is taxable income here. So you can choose to have the taxable bit in Australia, and that amount doesn't count to any limit, but it has 15 per cent tax taken out of it. If you only do a partial withdrawal, the growth component will have to be included on your tax return here and taxed at your marginal rates.

You'll also need to check on whether your Australian-based fund is a Qualifying Recognised Overseas Pension Scheme (QROPS) under UK regulations, and then weigh up the fees and returns. A financial adviser can help you on this. If it's not a QROPS fund, there'll be a 40 per cent tax penalty. However, an increasing number of funds are becoming qualified to meet the strict regulations on UK funds.

Q. I've separated recently and want to know whether I can share in my ex-partner's superannuation in the divorce settlement. I currently have no super in my own name, because I stopped work to look after the kids a decade ago.

Louise Biti, Head of Technical Services, Asteron:

The rules changed a few years ago to allow you to access your spouse's super. In the case of sharing in an ex-husband's super, he requests his fund to withdraw an amount and roll it over into your name. It sounds like a good idea, because you have super for retirement as shared savings, and it avoids some of the past complications such as being hit with tax. However, it could also mean that the remaining assets outside of super may be denied to you. So the first step is to see what the split involves in terms of the percentage of assets and who keeps what. You may not want to split the super; it's up to you. But you have the choice now!

Q. We're keen to get into the home market, and one way we could do that is through a 100 per cent fixed-rate, interest-only mortgage. I've also been reading about how, with the new super rules, we could be better off putting our home mortgage repayments into a fixed loan and not paying down the debt. Instead, we put the extra money into super and then pay the house off later with the lump sum — which has no tax on withdrawal if you retire after age 55. What are the pros and cons of this approach?

Anne-Marie Esler, Technical Research Manager, Centric Wealth:

There are many issues to consider before proceeding with this strategy, and the answer should be determined case-by-case.

A significant benefit of this super strategy comes in sacrificing your salary directly to super, so that instead of paying tax at your marginal tax rates, your contribution is subject to a 15 per cent contributions tax within the fund. Normally, your mortgage payments are made from your after-tax income, so a saving is made. A second advantage of this strategy is that you should be able to diversify your funds across a range of asset classes through your super fund, with the potential of generating a higher return with less risk. Investing all your money into one asset, such as your home, means you'll be at the mercy of rises and falls in the property market.

Having said that, this strategy could fall down in one respect: it's important that your superannuation contributions match the payments you'd normally have made to your mortgage—and that takes discipline!

Another disadvantage is that superannuation monies are 'preserved', which means you can't access your capital until you've permanently retired at age 55-plus—this could be a number of years away. So you may be depriving yourself of an additional source of savings. Unlike super, extra mortgage repayments made into an offset account are accessible should you need access to additional funds. An added advantage to making extra repayments into your mortgage is that you can use this equity to buy other assets—perhaps an investment property or shares.

This is not a strategy for the risk-averse, either. Remember that the return on your mortgage (in the case of a fixed home loan) is set, whereas the return on your superannuation funds will normally vary each year. In order for the strategy to work effectively, the return on your super needs to be at least equal to or greater than the interest rate on your loan. For example, if your interest rate is set at 8 per cent per annum, the after-tax return on your super fund needs to be at least this.

Lastly, you should also consider the emotional and psychological factors—think of how satisfying it will feel if you have worked hard and paid off your home loan prior to retirement!

Q. I'm still part of a self-managed super fund with my ex-husband. Recently he got engaged, and I'm wondering if I should exit the fund.

Louise Biti, Head of Technical Services, Asteron:[*]

All members of a self-managed fund must be trustees of the super fund. This means that all members are fully involved in and responsible for the fund's operations, and participate equally in the fund's decision-making processes. The trustees decide how to operate the fund, what investment strategy to choose and to whom they pay death benefits.

If you decide to keep your superannuation in the SMSF with your husband, you will both be trustees of the fund. How well this works may depend on how well you get on with your ex-husband. You need to consider if you still want to interact with him, and are comfortable with him having some control over decisions relating to your super. This could become more complicated if your ex-husband remarries and introduces his new wife as a member of the fund. The new wife would also become a trustee, and their combined votes could outweigh your own.

If you do continue in the self-managed fund, it may be important to ensure you have a binding death benefit nomination on your account (provided this is allowed under the fund's trust deed). This would ensure that you choose who receives your benefits in the event of your death, rather than allowing your ex-husband to be involved in this decision.

Before you take any action, you should seek the advice of a professional financial adviser who can help you understand your obligations as trustee of an SMSF and, if you decide to roll over your superannuation benefits, can help you choose a new fund.

[*] From 'Suddenly Super' by Julianne Dowling. This material first appeared in *Notebook:* magazine, March 2006.

Anne-Marie Esler, Technical Research Manager, Centric Wealth, adds:

Recent changes to legislation now make the process of separating your assets from your self-managed superannuation fund in the event of divorce a lot easier. From 1 July 2007, spouses who find themselves in a marriage breakdown will be able to transfer their assets, including direct share or property investments, from their SMSF to another complying superannuation fund without triggering a capital gains tax liability. This means you have the option of setting up a SMSF in your own name and transferring your existing assets without having to pay tax on any gains you may have made since the assets were purchased.

Q. I have my own business and I'm in my forties. What are the pros and cons of investing more in the business and less in super?

Louise Biti, Head of Technical Services, Asteron:[*]

Often, the mindset of small business-owners is that 'my business represents my super' and that building it up is a form of saving. But under the changes to super, there are now limits on how much you can contribute, so that's a major inhibiting factor for shovelling in money at a later date—you can't just sell the business and move the money over in one hit if it exceeds the limits.

From 2007–08, there's a cap of $150 000 on undeducted contributions in one year, so you'll have to make contributions in instalments. If you're under 65, though, you can use

---

[*] From 'Suddenly Super' by Julianne Dowling. This material first appeared in *Notebook:* magazine, March 2006.

the averaging provisions and bring forward the limits for two years into the current year—that takes you up to the $450 000 limit. If you do this, you can't contribute for three years afterward. You also have an extra $1 million limit for contributions from the sale of a small business, which gives you a bit more flexibility. Still, the limits mean you may need to contribute more regularly and have strategies in place.

The other change is to do with bankruptcy. A small business provides you with retirement savings and a livelihood, but what happens if you become bankrupt? It can happen through no fault of your own—say, if a major creditor goes bankrupt. Under the old rules, money saved in superannuation (up to the pension reasonable benefit limit of $1 238 440 in 2004–05) was protected in a bankruptcy situation. Now, that's changed. The upper limit has gone, and in a bankruptcy situation, you'll have to go to the courts and argue with the bankruptcy trustee about whether the contributions [to your business] have been part of a regular savings plan. Only regular contributions each year would be seen as a genuine retirement saving.

Superannuation shouldn't be neglected by small business owners. It provides:

- *Diversification.* It means you aren't relying on just one source (your business) to provide your retirement funding.
- *Some asset protection.* While this can't save your business, it does mean that any money you've put into super for your retirement won't be lost as long as you are regularly contributing.
- *Tax concessions.* As a business owner, you can either make personal deductible contributions to your super

fund (if you operate as a sole trader or in a partnership) or salary sacrifice to super (if you operate through a company or trust). Contributions are taxed at 15 per cent in the fund rather than being taxed as personal income at your marginal tax rate. If you're paying tax at the top rate of 48.5 per cent, that's a saving up to 33.5 per cent.

Again, the main disadvantage with superannuation is that the money is preserved. You generally won't be able to take any money out until you meet a condition of release, such as retirement after your preservation age (55 to 60, depending on your date of birth). So you need to be sure that any money you put into super is earmarked only for retirement.

I'd recommend that you discuss your situation in more detail with a professional adviser. An adviser can help you work out a balance between reinvesting into your business and building up superannuation that meets your needs.

Jane Rutter's souffle for one

'I don't know what I'll do for retirement', says creative powerhouse and single mother Jane Rutter. 'Being a musician, I plan to never retire!'

Jane's 2007 has been frenzied: she released a number-one classical CD, performed in back-to-back concerts—some requiring travel—wrote two books and, as a mother, was also conscious of making time for her son.

I'd love to have my mortgage paid off. But that said, I think it's everyone's birthright to be creative, and it's been my choice to have a different 'one-off' style of career. Freelance musicians frequently think about how to cope financially. Generating the kind of work that sustains my lifestyle is a concern!

She adds:

I have a rather pathetic amount of super, partly because my father encouraged me to invest my money into property. So far, I have my own home and a portion of the family farm. A couple of times I've invested in property and, mainly due to bad luck (and not hanging onto property long enough), made little profit. I think buying investment properties using the equity in your home can work well for people with double, regular incomes, but I found it a stressful and risky strategy, because my income fluctuates so much.

Single women, particularly the self-employed, are probably more likely to need the help of a financial coach and adviser on saving, investing and retirement, to ensure that the souffle goes in the right direction!

Souffle alternative: Jane Rutter's brilliant fruit tart

2 cups plain flour
2 cups brown sugar
2 cups butter
fruit in season, such as stone fruit, apples or pears

Mix the dry ingredients and 1.5 cups of butter into a dough. Grease a baking tray and push the dough into the tray to create a base and a ledge. Place the fruit on top, add the rest of the butter and more brown sugar, and bake until caramelised with syrup. Good luck—very easy and yummy!

Chapter 8
Investing: the Smorgasbord

> As you get older, you become more aware of planning and being sensible.
> —Kylie Jaye, serial entrepreneur

The statistics don't lie. Half of us will be divorced, and almost a quarter of us will never marry, so don't count on being part of a couple for your financial salvation! What comes out of your kitchen in the end is your responsibility. Even if you're part of a couple, you need to be on top of your recipe financially speaking, as it's very likely that you'll outlive your other half and kick on well into your early eighties.

At some point in everyone's life, they have surplus savings. Yet many women only ever think about buying property, and leave the rest of their money lurking in a term deposit or a high-yield account. There are lots of other investment choices that could possibly get better returns and growth. Self-proclaimed 'kick-arse chick' Kylie Jaye—the force behind Soclever and numerous other marketing and entertainment brands—says this is where the quality of advice counts for a lot. Kylie is quite conservative about her money, preferring to focus on property to date, but having advisers has helped her to look at different options that suit her situation and diversify her risks. She says, 'Often, it's the advisers behind successful people (who make it happen)'.

Home cookin' vs gastronomy: your risk profile

So how do you know what to do with your savings? What investments are likely to be best for you? The answer depends on your risk personality. Financial planners tend to assess this by giving you a questionnaire, but it's important that you come to terms with your appetite for risk yourself as well. Try taking an online risk-profile test on sites such as <www.anz.com> and <www.myrisktolerance.com> to get an initial idea. If you're part of a couple, keep in mind that the two of you may have a different risk profiles, different points of view and different levels of knowledge. It's helpful to know this upfront so you can take it into account in your investing plans.

A mismatch between your investments and your profile can be a problem. For example, in the days before the Financial Services Reform Act—under which financial advisers have to check your risk profile before they make any recommendations—working professional and mother of four Julie wound up with a highly aggressive product despite having a conservative profile: 'It was a $35 000 investment, which is a reasonable amount to lose, but a good lesson learned. It put me off investing, although I still have an adviser'.

All investments carry risk—even cash can erode due to inflation and fees. However, investments are generally considered to fall into four basic asset classes which carry different levels of risk: property, shares, fixed-interest investments and cash. High-quality shares, cash and fixed interest are 'defensive' assets; other shares and property are 'growth' assets. The difference between the two is what's called the 'risk and return' relationship—defensive assets have lower risk but also lower returns, whereas growth assets have higher risk and higher returns. Which investment types you choose depends on your goals, your time frame and whether you're after growth or the preservation of your money.

The key question is how long you've got to invest. Each asset class has a different time horizon for delivering returns, and to some extent, you can ride out ups and downs in your assets' values (called 'volatility') by holding on to them for a longish time. So, if you've got 10, 15 or 20 years ahead of you before retirement, growth assets like shares and property are recommended. But if you're about to retire, investing in shares may be a bad idea—especially if you haven't had previous experience with them. Then again, you also need to think about whether you're ready to stop work altogether; if you don't need to start drawing on your savings you might still want to keep some long-term investments. According to Putnam Investments, in the US, 35 per cent of retirees return to work either full-time or part-time. So think about where you're at and what your plans are.

Holding assets from the different classes—as part of your diversification—can also help smooth out your returns. Delma Newton, founder of Total Portfolio Management in Brisbane, comments:

> There's a tendency for people to stick to what they know about when it comes to money. Most people

aren't anti-diversification; sometimes, you just need to remind them that they don't have to consolidate everything in the same pool.

So that's the textbook answer. In life, the choices are not always clear-cut! To help you work out what investments might be for you, we're going to look at the most common investment options, managed funds and direct shares, plus when margin loans can be a useful strategy. We'll also look at the question of how best to save for your kids' education. The good news is that over the long term, good-quality shares and managed share funds have proved to be a good bet; they also have the advantage of providing a good long-term income stream that will almost pay for the cost of the investment. However, adviser Lisa Faddy of Majella Wealth Advisers warns that you should keep your expectations about future profits realistic: the sharemarket has done brilliantly over the past few years so you have to expect that, on average, returns will be lower over the next few.

Before we get into it, however, let's take a quick look at what may be your most important investment decision: choosing an adviser.

Consulting the food critics

So you've decided you need a financial adviser to help you through the trickier ins and outs of dealing with your money. How do you choose a good one? The Financial Planners Association of Australia and ASIC both have checklists on their websites and say that qualifications are important.

In order to set up a business a financial adviser must have an Australian financial services licence, but many advisers go on and study for a Certified Financial Planner qualification. It's a fairly arduous course—certified advisers have worked hard to gain up-to-date knowledge.

Ultimately, rapport with your adviser is vital. You might want to choose two or three advisers to interview to see who you're most comfortable with. But make sure you've done your homework before you meet them—you need to have analysed your spending budget, set short-term and long-term goals, and calculated your net worth.

All advisers, of course, charge fees, whether these are commission-based or time-based. Many prefer to charge a percentage on the funds they advise on, perhaps about 1 per cent. Again, compare a few different advisers and make sure you're happy with how much you're paying.

Lisa Faddy adds that when an adviser analyses your situation, choosing a fund or other investment is at the end of the process. The main focus should be on putting together a financial or investing strategy for you and understanding your tax and superannuation situation.

Managed funds

Many investors like managed funds (where a manager invests a pool of investors' funds) because they're easy. Like a set menu at a restaurant, all the choices are made for you by a professional. You just eat the end product! There are other benefits, too: it doesn't take much money to enter a fund; the investments tend to be more diversified than you could manage by yourself; and with their greater buying power, funds can access things you don't want to (or can't) invest in directly, such as international shares.

The set menu: how do managed funds work?

- To join a fund, you need to read its product disclosure statement, lodge an application form and buy units in the fund.
- You buy the fund's units at whatever their price is on the day of purchase. That price, multiplied by the number of units you bought, equals the value of your investment.
- Multi-sector funds invest in a range of assets (shares, property, and so on), and you can choose between the fund's investment streams, which are generally balanced, conservative and growth options.
- Single-sector funds focus on just one asset type — Australian shares, say — but may diversify within that asset class. That is, it may hold shares in companies in different areas of business, like resources companies, industrial companies and retailers.
- Funds charge a fee for management known as the management expense ratio (MER). There are also generally exit and entry fees.
- The fund's returns may be delivered as income or capital growth. Income is paid as a 'distribution', usually quarterly.

- The minimum investment in a fund is usually $1000, though some accept anything above $500 and allow automatic contributions of as little as $100 after that.

Sources: <www.mercerwealthsolutions.com.au> (under wealth information and fact sheets: 'A guide to understanding managed investments') and <www.ifsa.com.au> (Investment and Financial Services Association).

Which funds manager?

When it comes to funds manager selection, a good long-term track record is important. However, funds managers and fund structures do change, so a financial adviser who's kept on top of things can be handy. (They're kept informed by the research house reviews and ratings changes made by independent ratings houses like Lonsec and Morningstar.)

Passive or active funds?

Managed funds come in two main flavours: actively managed and passive or indexed funds. An indexed fund's investments match what's listed on a share index like the All Ordinaries or the S&P 100. Historically, indexes have achieved good returns over time, and indexing can smooth out the peaks and troughs in some asset classes in the long run. The other benefits of indexing are that the funds manager doesn't research which shares to buy and sell and when: meaning the fees for indexed funds are often lower. There's also less turnover and consequently, the transaction costs are lower.

Indexed funds can suit first-time investors or those with a small portfolio, because they offer quick, diversified exposure to the market. Another advantage is that there are a range of funds to invest in, so you if you prefer, you can focus on an area—say, small-cap companies—by choosing a fund that mirrors the relevant index. However, as your portfolio value increases, some experts argue that indexing is less relevant.

More and more financial planners (and DIY investors, especially those with self-managed super funds) like to have a mix of indexed and non-indexed funds. Lisa Faddy, for example, says that there are certain sectors that do better with active managers who select the stocks to buy and sell themselves. ANZ's Praveena Sharma comments, 'Indexing doesn't consider the sectors and stocks specifically, so that can be an issue. I use indexed funds when the market is volatile, but generally I'll pick some actively managed funds as well. Active managers can be very useful if a market goes down; I try to get a happy medium'. For further information about indexing strategies, take a look at <www.vanguard.com.au>, <www.statestreet.com.au> and <www.dimensional.com.au>.

Buying in

Advisers increasingly recommend that investors buy managed funds through either a 'platform'—an administration structure which is run and owned by a master trust—or a 'wrap', which is similar to a platform, but in which you retain beneficial ownership over the investments. The benefits of this are that the administration work is done for you and the funds are cheaper, as the fees are closer to wholesale charges the institutions pay. Your redemption requests (orders to sell fund units), for example, will be processed automatically, reducing time and paperwork. It can also cut down accounting fees.

Acquiring a taste for shares

> I got started at the age of 23, when I was working with a funds management group—that's how I saved a deposit. I put money into a managed fund and also bought shares. You had to go through an approved broker where I worked. Now, I wouldn't even know how to sell them if I wanted to!
> —Carly, 30, business manager

Does the idea of owning shares seem so *not* you? As one newcomer to a share club observes, 'The closest I've got to stock was in a cube'. With all the super talk, there's a view that shares outside of superannuation just don't cut it. But blue-chip and good-quality shares are easy to buy and sell (whereas it may take you ages to offload a property), give you tax credits if there are franked dividends and, in the case of high-yielding shares, may potentially provide better grossed-up returns (that is, tax credits plus the dividend return) than your term deposit.

Still, you do need to have a longer time horizon to ride out any price fluctuations—and even then there may be five-year cycles during which stocks don't do so well compared to, say, cash. You also need to select stocks carefully and diversify your portfolio across sectors to minimise your risk.

Bottom line, what are the five practical things you need in order to give shares a go?

1. *Money*...yes, but not necessarily heaps of it. Maybe dedicate a small set amount such as $2000 to $5000 to begin with. Remember that trading costs eat into your profit, so don't trade too often!

2. *Motivation to do a bit of maths with your calculator.* You'll need to work out some numbers on your stocks — such as the grossed-up returns, the dividend cover and the earnings growth.
3. *Mental effort.* There's no easy way around this — you've got to understand the jargon and concepts involved in the sharemarket. Read a fun book like Tracey Edwards' *Shopping for Shares*, check the latest ASX share guide booklet, or take a course (visit <www.asx.com.au> and the Australian Investors Association, <www.aia.org.au>, for more). Start reading the business sections of the daily press and the financial media too, but focus on the companies you want to know more about. It's also a good idea to run a pretend portfolio for a while, choosing companies, tracking their prices and getting into the habit of keeping dividend records and buying and selling records.
4. *The internet or a stock broker.* If you have less than $20 000 to invest, it's best to check out the large online brokers, such as E*Trade or CommSec, which charge less than a full-service broker. It's free to register, and you can then access some of their research and tools — watch lists are particularly useful in setting up a trial pretend portfolio. (CommSec and E*Trade also allow you to do a one-off trade without registering, which can be useful if you just want to sell the shares Aunt Millie left you or that you scored from a demutualisation.)
5. *Some research tools.* You can use your broker's free research, but if you're a DIY-er then you should

consider buying research as well. Some popular research sites are <www.fatprophets.com.au>, <www.aspecthuntley.com.au>, <www.intelligentinvestor.com.au>, <www.stockdoctor.com.au>, <www.wealthwithin.com.au> and <www.aegis.com.au>.

Shareholders Down Under

The 2006 Australian Securities Exchange share-ownership survey revealed a drop in the percentage of investors holding direct and indirect shares through managed funds — from 55 per cent to 46 per cent. However, the majority of Australians still hold shares through their super funds.

The typical investor is 49 years old, with an average household income of $76 000. The average share portfolio was worth $190 600 and the average share trade was $14 200, with shareholders making eight trades a year. But look, it's all about averages, so no one person necessarily fits that bill!

How many stocks?

Often early starters want to work out what the perfect portfolio size is. That is, how many stocks should they hold? All Money Matters founder and financial coach Louise Brogan — a highly experienced share trader and former stockbroker — believes that everyone is different, but with a 'buy and hold' portfolio, the minimum number would be typically about three stocks:

> Most people I work with start feeling overwhelmed with more than five to eight stocks.

With a full-service broker, the client works out the portfolio they want to work towards, sets up a cash management trust (CMT) account, and then regularly deposits amounts into this. The broker recommends a number of stocks that meet the client's criteria, say a dozen, and the client picks, say, five or six. They will usually be spread over the market sectors.

The client has an agreement with the broker that once the CMT has reached a certain dollar amount — whatever is going to give them a reasonable brokerage rate — the broker will purchase that dollar amount of shares in one of their pre-selected stocks. This continues over the years, so their portfolio grows. [People generally] also put extra amounts into the CMT if they get them — tax refunds, gifts, etc.

Share clubs

Share clubs are one way some women choose to get their share-investing P-plates — pooling their resources and knowledge with friends and limiting their risk by staking a smaller amount of capital.

Martha Saw and seven friends, who now range in age from 41 to 55 up, began an investment share club group after meeting for drinks every second Friday night at a Canberra hotel. The Friday Investment Girl's Group (FIGG) began with a buy-in pool of funds that was then topped up by monthly contributions — $50 each at first; later $150.

> We wanted to tap into our girl power and learn something new. We used an online broker and also

subscribed to *The Intelligent Investor*, trialled one or two [newsletters], and then used our own research; we found the ASX site really useful and sometimes the investment media too.

We never spent more than $4000 on one purchase. We went through different phases where we'd concentrate on cheaper stocks because 'small gains are good gains', and then we'd buy blue chips, but the discussion would sway from one stock to another. So then we developed a pro forma approach on buying a stock. If you had an idea for a stock, then you had to provide an argument as to why buy.

Knowing when to sell a stock and not laying blame was difficult, she says. 'Listening and valuing each person's suggestions and buying at the right price was also tricky.' Still, the women recently dissolved FIGG and walked away with $10 000 each and some tax credits from dividends along the way as a 'nice little bonus'.

Other share club secrets:

- Have a clear trading structure to cover liability and protect funds in the event of any potential conflicts. Share clubs often use a partnership.
- Be prepared to do extra administration for the tax year. For every share you buy there'll be at least four pieces of paper to handle. There are also logs for dividends and transactions to keep for tax purposes — although you can print off your transactions from an online broker.
- Take care that you don't breach the rules under the Financial Services Reform Act, which says that no-one

can give financial advice without being licensed. That means the strongest person in the group can't make all the recommendations and decisions about the portfolio! Ensure that there are equal inputs into stock selection; shared, rotated responsibilities; and ideally, members with similar levels of financial nous.
- Martha says that the friendship factor can complicate money issues. Automatic monthly debits can be a good option for contributions, so that nobody is behind on payments.

Jane Toohey's share recipe

Brisbane-based Jane Toohey, co-owner of marketing consultancy Marketing Angels, has been interested in shares for over 15 years. Jane has a diverse approach to her portfolio and also has property investments and managed funds. A year ago, she decided to redeem $60 000 from her managed funds to invest into direct shares. Now, she's got three separate share portfolios with very different strategies and risk levels.

> I've had a strategy for shares over 15 years. But the transfer of more money from my managed funds into direct shares was prompted by a plan that my broker had developed for the children's education. Direct investing means I'm happy to take the decision rather than let someone else take it for me.

She invested her extra $60 000 under advice from her broker and was thrilled to find that her portfolio went up by $25 000 in three months. Of course, the March 2007 drop in the market also lost her money, but she says that even at the lowest point it was only $10 000.

Jane's three portfolios are her self-managed super fund, where she takes the lowest risk (buy and hold shares); the children's portfolio (shares in a range of high-growth companies, geared through margin lending); and her own personal portfolio, which carries the highest risk and invests in small-cap and start-up companies. She adds that she's secure in the knowledge that if the costs of her investment loans go up (due to rate rises), they can be covered from her growing business cash flow.

> Right now, I'm into building wealth rather than taking profit. When it comes to a margin loan, your earnings must pay for that loan. You can't have speculative shares, and remember, the tax-deductibility of negative gearing is not the main justification for doing it! I'm also fully insured. That's important.

Jane's cooking tips

- Get the right advice and don't be held back by your fears. There are 10 people out there who'll say 'Don't do it!' for every one person who encourages you.
- At times, I may decide it's better to sit tight on my share portfolio, particularly when the market becomes volatile! If the portfolio's working well then don't tinker with it just for the sake of change. Maybe consider adding stocks to the portfolio, but don't change what you've got unless you really have to.

Margin lending

A lot of women are scared of gearing, says ANZ Financial Planner Carla Chambers. Nevertheless, she adds, 'Women are getting more interested in gearing'.

> We can now offer a margin loan to a 'balanced' investor which gives them an opportunity to amplify their returns; previously, they were only suitable for investors with an 'aggressive' risk profile.
>
> When the markets are high or volatile, a regular geared savings plan can work well: the investor enters the market a little at a time, rather than with one lump sum. This allows 'dollar cost averaging' which means you buy in at different prices instead of at, say, an all-time high.

Margin loans work well in a rising market. If there's a downturn in the value of your investments, and your loan amount exceeds the security on your investments, your lender may 'call' for you to top up your loan funds. The other issue is that gearing magnifies your losses as well as your gains.

Just remember that whatever the interest rates are, you have to clear that hurdle in your profits; loans still have to be repaid even when investments fluctuate in value. Of course, tax benefits may soften the blow—if your marginal tax rate is high and interest rates are low, a margin loan may appeal.

Delma's all geared up

At 36, Delma Newton is an active investor. It's no surprise that she's confident about her abilities—she's a financial planner with her own boutique financial services firm. Delma and her partner are both self-employed and have a mortgage. They've used margin loans across their managed funds, with a few funds rated as aggressively high-risk and the gearing increasing that risk. She warns:

> Not everyone can sustain that level of risk. Given that we're still young, we don't need to worry if the market is down by 20 per cent, but if you're closer to retiring you can't afford to do that.

In order to show how a margin loan could work, Delma's done the sums for 'Lara', our hypothetical investor. Lara has an income of $80 000, is borrowing $50 000 for an investment in managed funds, and is paying 40 per cent marginal tax in 2006–07. We assume that the income on the funds will be 15 per cent per annum, averaging out at 8 per cent a year over five years.

So Lara's net income looks like this:

Income	$80 000
Tax and Medicare levy	($20 300)
Net income	**$59 700**

If Lara takes out a margin loan with an interest rate of 8.95 per cent and an income of 8 per cent yearly, that will work as follows:

Income	$80 000
Income from portfolio	$4 000
Interest	($4 475)
Taxable income	*$79 525*

Tax and Medicare levy	($20 103)
Net income	**$59 422**

So after tax, Lara needs to fund $278 per annum to maintain the investment—not such a big ask in that year. But she needs to have the right risk profile and to be able to withstand any variations on those numbers.

In 2007–08, the tax thresholds drops from 40 to 30 per cent, while the out-of-pocket gap that Lara will need to fund increases:

Income	$80 000
Tax and Medicare levy	($19 600)
Net income	**$60 400**

With margin lending, assuming interest rates of 8.95 per cent and income of 8 per cent, the numbers run as:

Income	$80 000
Income from portfolio	$4 000
Interest	($4 475)
Taxable income	*$79 525*
Tax and Medicare levy	($19 650)
Net income	**$59 875**

Now, Lara has to fork out $325 per annum to maintain her investment. And if she prefers to invest in Australian shares, then the income return is likely to be lower. 'A more realistic income return for Australian shares long term is around 5 per cent', says Delma. 'Over a 20-year period, Australian shares returned around 12 per cent—and this includes both capital growth and income'. So, from a tax perspective:

Income	$80 000
Tax and Medicare levy	($20 300)
Net income	**$59 700**

With a margin loan, assume the interest rate is 8.95 per cent and income 5 per cent, and the new outcome is:

Income	$80 000
Income from portfolio	$2 500
Interest	($4 475)
Taxable income	$78 025
Tax and Medicare levy	($19 480)
Net income	**$58 545**

So, after tax, our Lara needs to fund $1155 a year to maintain the investment. You can see how the gap jumps up with a lower marginal tax rate and lower return; Lara might think twice about the extra cash flow required here!

Baking an education pie

One of the common reasons for investing is the kids' education at secondary and/or tertiary levels. Many families wonder about the best way to save and invest for this. You probably don't want to let it dominate your investing life at the expense of other financial goals, of course! After all, there are lots of other options if you can't afford the full six years of private secondary schooling.

Some families limit private school to Years 11 and 12 only. Others invest elsewhere and fund education fees as they go along or choose a good public school topped up with private coaching. Whatever you choose, saving for schooling is a bit like saving for old age. You have a long time frame and you don't want to lose your money, but you want to make the most of your savings. There's also tax to consider on the returns—it'll be charged at your marginal tax rate (MTR) or at the rate of the person whose name is on the investments.

Usually, planners suggest that it's best to put the lowest MTR person's name on the investment, unless you're gearing. However, bear in mind that the family's lowest income-earner may change tax status at some point—they may become more highly paid or return to the workforce—don't forget to factor these changes into your strategy.

There are pros and cons for all types of investment when you're saving for education. It just depends upon your situation, says Lisa Faddy, co-founder of Majella Wealth Advisers:

> Certain managed funds will be better suited to education needs. These include tax-deferred or lower turnover index funds. There are also education bonds which have tax-paid returns, but these may be less flexible than more 'traditional' managed funds. What we generally recommend is diversification. So if you have a longer time horizon, that could give you more options for investment.
>
> One strategy that's favoured by high-earning couples with an aggressive risk outlook is to gear into managed funds and make regular contributions alongside loaned amounts. This can be done via a margin loan or an equity loan. The advantage of

tax-deductible debt effectively reduces the cost of your borrowings and boosts your returns. It would also increase your losses if the market falls, of course, so you need to weigh up the short-term risks. But longer term, it could still significantly grow your capital.

Lisa suggests that grandparents avoid putting investments in their grandchildren's names; tax levels for children are up to 66 per cent over earnings of $416—although they can effectively earn up to $1333 with the low-income tax rebate. She says, 'Better to set up separate accounts where you name the account after the child but the beneficial ownership remains with the lower tax-paying adult'.

The pros and cons of different ingredients

Managed funds

Pros

- Tax will be payable in the hands of the investor (usually one of the parents). This works well if one parent isn't working or has a lower marginal tax rate. If the fund invests in Australian shares, there may be franked dividends receivable.
- You have the option of making automated monthly payments.

Cons

- Management expense ratios average between 0.2 per cent and 2 per cent, though wholesale funds can be accessed for less on a platform (e.g. 0.7 per cent to 0.56 per cent platform plus adviser fee).
- You may also have to pay entry fees on each contribution, depending upon the rebate policy.

Direct shares
Pros
- There are virtually no administration costs.
- 'Growth'-oriented companies may be better, as they retain profits rather than pay out dividends, which means less tax.
- Shares are best owned in the name of the lower tax payer.

Cons
- Direct shares are probably the most volatile investment class to hold, and you may not pick the best time to sell. It may not be efficient to sell off small parcels of shares each year to pay school fees.
- You may be less likely to treat shares as a regular savings plan, and you need time and knowledge to select and maintain your portfolio.
- If you're only investing a small amount, you can only diversify across a small number of stocks.

Mortgage offset
Pros
- There are no tax implications—this is possibly the cleanest and most effective alternative.

Cons
- This isn't permitted if the mortgage is on an investment property.
- There's a temptation to spend money on other things if your funds are accessible.

Bank account
Cons
- Your money is secure.
- At-call accounts are readily accessible.

Cons
- Keeping money in a bank account has little or no tax benefit, unless you're on a low income. The risk is low, but so is the return; and fixed-term accounts can have 'break' fees if you exit early.
- Again, there's a temptation to spend money on other things if your funds are accessible.

Education plans

Pros
- These are similar to insurance bonds—tax is paid at 30 per cent.
- The benefits are focused more toward tertiary education.

Cons
- The fees can be high. You can take out money, but there could be penalties if it's before the target date.
- Education plans may be restricted to tertiary or secondary senior years.

Insurance bonds or friendly society bonds

Pros
- These are tax-paid products (at the company tax rate of 30 per cent), which is good if both parents are working and on a tax rate higher than 30 per cent (the 40 per cent rate kicks in at $75001).
- They offer some level of investment choice, so you can opt for a higher risk/return.
- You have the option of making regular payments and still maintaining 'tax-paid' status.

Cons
- If you access the money within 10 years, additional tax may be payable.

- Investment choices are usually limited to one manager, and the entry, exit and ongoing fees can be high.
- These bonds are only offered by limited number of companies.

© CPA Australia. Reproduced with permission.

Investment recipe: Jane Toohey's classic spag bol

First, open a bottle of red and pour a glass for yourself. Then, use your food processor to finely chop 4 brown onions and 3 cloves of garlic, and heat some olive oil in a big pot with 2 bay leaves and a good sprig of rosemary. When the oil gets hot, put the onions and garlic in and cook until translucent.

Process a tub of semi-sun-dried tomatoes, a handful of olives and 250g of prosciutto, add it into the pan and top up your wineglass. Once the ingredients look half-cooked, add 2 kg of mince—a bit at a time so it browns evenly. Then process 2 cups of mushrooms, add them and cook for another couple of minutes. Remember to keep stirring, so the mix doesn't catch in the pan. Then add 5 tins of tomatoes (the 400g tins) and 3 tubs of tomato paste. Depending on how wet it looks, add a cup of chicken stock.

Place 4 to 6 pieces of parmesan rind in the pot, lower the heat to a simmer, and cover and cook for an hour. Check the sauce and stir it every 15 minutes so nothing gets stuck on the bottom. Once it's thickened, take it off the heat.

Cook your pasta and drain it. Toss some olive oil and fresh chopped basil into the pasta, dollop the sauce on top and serve with a green salad!

Chapter 9
The Catering Conundrum

> *Women with heart bring a lot to the business environment.*
> —Bella Serventi, restaurateur

There's such a rush of women to small and micro businesses, it's enough to make you wonder if you shouldn't be 'ordering what she's having'! But when you look at the split between men and women joining the entrepreneurial ranks, you can see that despite the noise, fewer women take up the business challenge. Swinburne University's research actually shows that the female/male ratio within early stage business ownership participation has declined dramatically, from 70 per cent in 2004 to 53 per cent in 2005. Swinburne research notes:

> An increase in female participation in Australia would lead to significant economic growth and competitive advantage on an international scale. We need to identify relevant political initiatives to encourage females to begin and sustain new businesses.

Learning from the chefs

Every business is different, and there's no one path to zen. If you've started or want to start your own biz and make it a success, doing lots of reading and research will help give you an edge—but for the time-poor it can be a stretch. We often have a mountain of reading associated just with the current daily grind; weekend newspapers and maybe a novel are about all most women can manage on top of that!

Fortunately, there's another way: learning some cooking strategies from the master chefs. Business owners love war stories and sharing what they've learnt with like-minded people. Ideally, every entrepreneur should try to find a mentor to bounce ideas off who can help them take a shortcut to success.

Entrepreneur Sally Wheat, who at the time of writing was launching a niche spa concept with venture capital backing, is looking for a local mentor after studying the spa industry in the US and Europe. She believes that the Americans are way ahead when it comes to peer support:

> They love to help and are totally engrossed by the motivational movement and getting everyone into win–win situations. One New York owner even opened up her books for me, she was so willing to help!

In the rest of this chapter, we're going to get a little mentoring from some very successful Australian businesswomen who are also keen to see others do well.

Starting up: swim gal Justine Harrison

Justine and husband Jud launched a swim school at the end of 2006, and it's making a big splash! The couple are popular with local families, and the number of kids attending lessons has hit 70, with more on the waiting lists. Jud's background—his dad had a swim school—and his history as a water-polo champion make him entirely suited to this enterprise, and he's at ease with the kids and parents. Justine says, 'Jud does all the coaching. He's tried to convince me to get my coaching certificate then hop in the pool and work with him, but I prefer to stay dry! I've been able to do all our design work, because that's my field, as well as the accounts and administration'.

However, both Justine and Jud are working full-time, and adding this part-time enterprise to their daily routine is exhausting. Justine says their biggest problem is time management: Mondays to Thursdays are full on with work and swim coaching, and they have to factor their two young daughters into the mix as well!

New-restaurant rules

Accountant Michelle Pearce, director of Face Chartered Accountants, regularly advises small business start-ups and has these suggestions for Justine and Jud and others like them:

- Consider whether you're running a business or doing a hobby. If you're running a business, then the income you generate is taxable and the costs you incur are deductible. If what you're doing is just a hobby, then you won't be taxed on the income but the costs incurred aren't tax deductible either.

- You need to make sure the idea for your business is really feasible. Your business plan helps you assess and define the product or service you are selling; who your competitors are; and what your strengths, weaknesses, opportunities and threats are. A business plan is a good move—it forces you to put your thoughts on paper in a structured way.
- Do you require finance to start up your business? Or do you have the financial capacity to stop full-time employment and run your new enterprise? You should ideally prepare financial budgets to make sure you can survive the first 12 months, when your business is in its infancy. You need to also assess what your establishment costs will be—for example, office or shop fit-outs and equipment.
- Consider what legal structure you want to operate your business in. There are four main types: sole trader, partnership, company or trust. The most common progression for small business is from sole trader to company. The costs of setting up a small business as a sole trader are fairly minimal; it's better to gauge how the business is going before you commit to a more permanent structure. However, if you're operating your business in a high-risk

industry (property development, for example), then you may want to consider using a company from the start, to protect your assets.
- You'll need to apply for the appropriate tax registrations. At a minimum, you need a tax file number and an Australian Business Number (ABN). These can be applied for online at the Australian Business Registration website (<www.abr.gov.au>) The ABN needs to go on your invoices—otherwise your customers/clients are required to withhold 47 per cent tax on your behalf and remit it to the ATO.
- If you're not using your personal name to trade under, then you should register a business name. Each state has different places to do that, usually through the consumer affairs or small business departments. Do a search online, and don't forget to check the ASIC website to make sure the name you want is not already in use.
- If your annual business income is over $55 000 per year, then you'll need to register for GST and charge your customers an additional 10 per cent. You'll also need to complete Business Activity Statements and lodge them with the ATO either monthly or quarterly.
- Make sure you have all the relevant business insurances and licenses for your operations. The insurance essentials are public and product liability insurance and professional indemnity

insurance. Speak to other people in your industry to make sure you have all the required registrations and licenses.
- You need to maintain accurate records of your finances. Under tax law, you're required to keep records for five years, including all sales, purchases, payments to employees and other business payments. You might consider using an accounting program such as MYOB for this. Also, it's much better to set up a separate bank account for your business, rather than operating through your personal account.
- If you're running your business from home, you should find out what expenses you can claim, such as electricity and council rates. If you decide to claim the interest relating to the mortgage on your home, be aware that these deductions will expose part of your home to capital gains tax.
- Protect your intellectual property: make sure your idea can't be copied or stolen.
- If you're going into business with someone else, make sure you have a legal agreement which covers things like profit sharing, contributions to the business, the ability of new parties to enter, and exit strategies.
- Finally, make sure you build relationships with an accountant, a lawyer, a business banker and an insurance broker. These professionals will assist you in growing your business.

Taking care of (personal) business

Women tend to neglect their personal fortunes in the early stages of a business because so they're so frantically focused on this one major thing. The personal funds are often sacrificed for the 'greater good' of reinvestment into the business — goodbye, market salary and taking out dividends!

It's important that women encourage each other to pay more attention to their own affairs, like super and investments. Because let's face it, the goose that lays the golden eggs may not be around forever.

There's a huge opportunity cost for letting your new plaything take over to the exclusion of everything else. In the early stages (under two or three years), if the rewards aren't flowing you're probably wondering if it's all worth it. But down the track, when they do, you're likely to regret that you didn't get more out of it for yourself.

Unless you have an angel or a venture capitalist behind you, it's common to lag behind when it comes to financing your business in the start-up phase. There are obvious reasons. Getting a bank overdraft for a business under two years old is generally very hard because financiers want to see audited tax returns. To cover any cash shortfalls, new owners are forced to dip into their own family funds or rack up expenses on credit cards.

The point is: don't do this for long! Work on the relationship with your bank and maintain some pressure on them to give you a better deal. After all, they'll be enjoying the ride when the good times roll.

Empire-builder: Anne McKevitt[*]

Anne McKevitt is a legendary serial entrepreneur who runs 22 businesses, counsels large organisations on cultural change, and helps other great entrepreneurs get to the next stage of growth. She's also in demand as a business-school lecturer. Her paid-members-only site <www.milliondollarplusclub.com> offers a high level of mentoring.

Anne epitomises the story of a girl succeeding against the odds. First she talked her way into working with iconic British hairdresser John Frieda. Then, after a horrific car accident left her with spinal damage, she went on to launch an interior design business. That evolved into an empire of different books, brands and products and gave her a taste for serial entrepreneurship. Anne says there are definitely gender differences in entrepreneurship:

> The hardest thing with women is too much multi-tasking. What I think succeeds is laser focus. With each business, you need a clear start, middle and end.

Anne also believes that time management is critical — often there's a buffet of opportunities, and entrepreneurs fritter away their energies on the lesser ones:

> Most [owners] have terrible time management skills and a poor ability to say no. Sometimes, you need to put things on the backburner. On the whole, entrepreneurs can suffer from seeing too much opportunity.

[*] First appeared as 'Secrets of a Self-confessed Serial Entrepreneur' by Julianne Dowling, *Vive* magazine, April/May 2007, p. 104.

It's vital, she adds, to be able to weed out the good ideas from the bad, and not to get too emotionally attached to a business—unless you want to remain just a manager. While you don't have to have a background in that business to make money, you should consider leveraging your experience within it 'or know you have found something that is a real cash cow and is working really fast'. She explains, 'You can be passionate about making money, but you don't need to be passionate about the thing that makes money'.

For instance, Anne says one business that she has little background in or empathy for is websites for medical e-books and courses. Yet it's proved highly profitable, and what started as a test run of five sites has built up to 200 sites. Another was a stationery business, which she sold almost as soon as it launched, 'because the larger players could see us as competitors. An entrepreneur is usually innovative, and can see an opportunity and make it happen...but always sees a clear exit strategy'.

Restaurant gal: Bella Serventi

Bella Serventi says that the year she spent on the box as a contestant in *My Restaurant Rules* taught her about managing a high-profile, high-turnover business fast. In the series, the challenge was to make the business work in a very short time frame; Bella and her business partner Evan steered their Sydney restaurant to a $1.2 million turnover in just a few weeks.

At 24, this girl has had a rocket ride to the top, but given her academic credentials—a master's in marketing—it's no surprise that she's star material. Bella and Evan's post-TV restaurant is Pink Salt in Double Bay. Bella loves her life but is looking for a new challenge as well. She's already thinking about expanding their brand into the Hong Kong market. Here are her answers to a few important money questions.

How do you create a work/life balance?

My biggest goal is life balance. I know I'm a poor boss and make poor decisions when I'm tired, so our goal is to have more downtime. I also know that I'm an emotional spender if I'm really tired. So I divide my personal and public life very strictly. In the business, I'm very detail-oriented and I want to know the flow of work and who I'm delegating to.

How do you avoid cash-flow mismanagement?

We follow a strict philosophy of controlling everything and running a tight ship, and that's why we've got so far. We're the only ones to touch the tills. Even today, if there's a cash bill then it has to come to us. That's one way we manage security and keep a handle on numbers and the consistency…We never take money out of the till either. If I need money, I'll go to my wallet. We also invest in security cameras.

What advice do you have for others planning a start-up?

I don't feel that I can give advice, but whether you're running a beauty salon or a HR company, it's important to look at it as a business. If you try to do everything and do nothing well, then it will reflect on the business. Leaving it to others takes a certain amount of trust.

The other thing to learn in business is to recover from crises quickly. Being emotional, I have a tendency to take things to heart—and that makes the business great too. But you need to recover [from the blows]… it's upsetting when someone leaves, but that's life. Positive thinking is important, and when there's a crisis you have to learn to swallow it, and think that you can do it better next time. If you don't, it stunts the growth of the business. You need to recognise that every day is a new one.

Are you happy with what you've achieved financially?
Money-wise, I'm happy! I know how hard we work and that you have to work harder to maintain what you've achieved. I'm part of the generation that wants more… and you keep jumping for those opportunities!

What money lessons did you get from your family?
My father is an old-fashioned Italian man, and he's strict with business. There are six children in our family, and we're all ambitious. He sacrificed a lot to send us to private schools and cover the tertiary education costs. My mother is the opposite, and that balance gave us a youthful philosophy: to give it back with heart because it's also your life. If you work hard and are hard on yourself, it's important to love what you do.

What about your personal money habits?

I've always had someone with strong financial expertise—either Dad or a partner—and I've always asked them to help me keep in check. I sometimes think I have the right to be spendthrift, and I don't apply the same rules to my personal life as my business life. I feel I work hard and I know my disposable income, so that's what I go with.

You need to look after yourself; sometimes I do have arguments with my partner about that. For the first time, I don't have a boundary on what I can spend [on daily things]. If I have that massage or a dinner on my day off, I don't look at the bill. Of course, if I had more time to shop and play then I'd probably be wary... but I don't really have time to spend it!

Bella's biz recipe

- Stay on top of the cash flow.
- Be honest with yourself, know your strengths and weaknesses and delegate where you can.
- Recover from a crisis quickly; let it go.
- Be prepared to work hard in the early stages but take time to recharge.
- It's okay to not have all the answers; every day is different.

Clean gal: Bex Gold

Brisbane-based Bex Gold, 29, happily admits she's a clean freak:

> I clean the house every day before I start work. I use this time to get my thoughts together and once the house is clean there are no distractions. If you clean regularly, it's never such a big job, and if I rush I can have everything done in 20 minutes.

What separates Bex from the rest of the world's cleaning whizzes is that she went on to create her own luscious-smelling cleaning range, aptly named Cinderella. It's rapidly moved from a boutique brand to a fast-moving consumer item, after supermarket giant Coles agreed to include it in their national distribution network. The key is to have a differentiated product, says Bex:

> Cinderella doesn't contain petroleum distillates and is based on plants; that's important because I live on an acreage property. I've also got cute packaging and fragrances. When I was launching, a US competitor had a $15 price point, which I think is a hard sell. So I took the key attributes and turned it over into a volume product.

As well as having a great idea, a unique formula and a drive to expand, Bex has a family of businesspeople right behind her:

> Dad is a bank of knowledge and Mum does small property developments; both of them have terrific skills. We talk shop every day; I love what we do and it's part of our family life.

Bex says smart time management is also critical to her business. She has a volume product that needs to expand quickly, and is planning her moves into the Asian and trans-Tasman markets. Given that she has limited marketing funds during the start-up phase, she's learning to stretch her dollar creatively and use below-the-line strategies, as well as redesigning her packaging to freshen up the brand's image.

> I don't have an exit strategy yet—right now it's my baby and I have a target to reach. Once I get there, I'll think about it. I don't want to go public, but who knows?

What's the key thing you've learned about money in your business so far? What about your own money?

> Cash flow, cash flow, cash flow. Planning, forecasting and ensuring fallback reserves are essential in both my business and personal money management.

How has this affected your decisions about the future?

> Each expansion and marketing activity has to be costed through and budgeted for. It's frustrating that you can't throw budget on fabulous advertising that can't guarantee reach and effectiveness, but it does force me to be creative.

What's the biggest financial challenge for the business?

> I'll need to change the way the business is structured to enter some overseas markets at the speed I want, because the business's ability to fund some of these entries doesn't stack up.

Do you pay yourself a market rate income?

I'm still in the growth stage of a volume business, so I'm not quite up to market rate!

Do you contribute super?

I have in the past at the 15 per cent rate and supplemented with tax-deductible forestry investments.

Do you have a self-managed super fund?

No—I haven't had the resources to structure and maintain a SMSF effectively.

How do you handle your personal finances generally? Are you happy with how they're going?

Getting a new business up off the ground calls for sacrifice, but I've been fortunate that I've had family support. Both company and personal expenditure is controlled and tracking in the right direction!

What are your money goals?

A healthy, diversified investment portfolio, a growing, cash-flow positive business and a personal cash flow that allows for a couple of life's luxuries!

How would you rate yourself on personal and business financial management?

I'm very structured and aware of inflows and outflows. A lot is tied up in the business—that's a risk, but risks make you work harder!

Do you use a financial planner?

I get a lot of business advice from my family, but I have a good accountant too.

Bex's biz recipe

- Plan and forecast — know your best-case and worst-case scenarios.
- Know your risks and understand your exposure before you commit.
- Know your growth and exit strategies. Sometimes things in business move fast, and you don't want to miss an opportunity.
- Negotiate and shop around. It can be hard to find the real price of things when you start in a new industry, but the right price can make all the difference.
- Keep your books and cash-flow records current.

Organising gal: Carol Posener

As a professional organiser, Carol Posener has observed the effects of cleaning up and de-cluttering on the lives of her clients firsthand:

> Clutter can be about protecting yourself with stuff. Clutter is negative energy, too — no wonder you don't want to be near it. It feels negative and confused. That's why it's good to do seasonal reviews. I purposely maintain my life and keep order so I can work. If I've got stuff everywhere, it's a distraction.

It's an area most of us want to improve: Carol's made a highly successful business out of showing people how to organise their time and space better. Her business, Get Organised, is a concierge service for people who want help managing their lives, and also offers corporate training sessions on improving systems and time management. As a pioneer of the industry in Australia, Carol has written a best-selling book (also called *Get Organised*) and now trains aspiring consultants.

How did you finance your business?

I funded it as I went, and probably struggled because of that; I should have gone to a bank. My overheads were low because I worked from home and the costs were minimal. I even ran training programs from home.

Do you pay yourself a market rate?

It's only in the past two years that I've been able to make a decent living; it's been a hard slog. Now, it's good to have my finances under control and have different income streams happening. I'd like to add more consultants, because the business could be incredible. Franchising is also on the cards, and I may look at a partner or financier to take it to a new level.

Training is a major focus. As well as consultants, I train both corporate clients and the general public on organising their lives, whether at work or home.

What's helped drive your growth?

After several years into my business, I realised that I needed to do more. So I did a workshop through the state's New Enterprise Incentive Scheme (NEIS). That six-week course showed me how to prepare a business plan and look at all areas of operation, including financials, marketing and administration; it gave me a picture of how things should run. I started managing everything more professionally, from trademarking to protect my business name, to fine-tuning my forms and even working on my presentation skills.

Is a business plan essential?

Doing a business plan was an eye-opener; the lecturers gave us a deadline of five weeks so I began on the first day of the course...trying to get really clear about my business, my markets, my clients. The plan needs to be redone every one to two years to keep the business moving forward—I've met all my plan objectives.

What about advisers?

My accountant gives me feedback every quarter; he also gives me goals for revenue and profitability. If I hadn't found that guy, I wouldn't be where I am now. He came through my sister and her husband, who have a highly successful international business.

Are you happy with how the business is tracking?

It took me two years to make money, but if you're clever about it you can develop opportunities to give you an income stream right from the start. That's why I want to impart knowledge—to save people who are entering the industry now from that. There are mistakes that I've made during the past 13 years that you can avoid, that will hook you into the right income stream right from the start...

What's your consultancy rate and how did you choose it?

When I started my rate was $25 per hour, but now it ranges between $75 and $150 per hour. I have a range of prices to suit the services offered. I don't do secretarial work. We're not cleaners: we're organisers. In the beginning, that was hard, because people used to see the role as a glorified cleaner. Confidentiality was another issue: people wouldn't refer me because they didn't want their friends to know that they were disorganised! The outsourcing trend has helped overcome that fear. It's more acceptable now for people to bring in help; it doesn't mean you're a loser if you haven't got time. Sometimes, of course, clients are really organised and just want to stay that way, or they want to get a benchmark on what they're doing. Now, I get referrals frequently.

What are your financial goals?

Continue to invest in shares, art...or property. I used to work for a stockbroker; I was a money-market dealer, and ran the fixed-interest and money-market desk. I had that background, studied at the Securities Institute of Australia for four years and also worked in a bank. And I entered those careers even though I'm not good at maths!

I have a share portfolio and handle it myself. I'm quite interested in China and the possibilities of investing there. Recently, I bought an Indigenous artwork. I'm keen to do more of that.

How do you recover money owing to you?

I realised quickly that if I didn't ask for payment up-front from clients then it could be an issue. If you're disorganised, then you may lose the bill and forget to pay.

By taking that approach I've never had a debtors issue; corporates may be slower but they will eventually pay. On the creditor side, keep communication open if you can't afford to pay immediately. If I wanted to do advertising, then I might negotiate to pay off the total in instalments. That's what I do for insurance.

Carol's biz recipe

- Keep tabs on your cash flow and watch your bills; monitor things every few days and don't let a week go by where you haven't looked at them. I work maybe two months ahead, so ensuring my income flows is really crucial. I didn't do that initially, but now I have a bookkeeper and use MYOB, and that makes a difference.
- Stick with your gut feeling; I was way ahead with my ideas and didn't realise that there was a growing movement in the US. If I'd gone

along with the view that there was no money in it, then I wouldn't have got anywhere. It was my gut instinct that kept me going, because the business idea was unique and I could see the need everywhere.

Where to find mentors

If you're looking for a mentor, there are a number of websites and government programs that can help.

The Australian Businesswomen's Network (ABN) has an online mentoring program for women under 35. MentorNet is a six-month training program which uses podcasts, online questionnaires, and other teaching tools to help women in regional areas and those with no support networks. Visit <www.abn.org.au> for more, or call 1300 720 120 for applications. The program costs $935 and is sponsored by the federal government.

Executives can visit <www.networkcentral.com.au> for mentors relationships and networking events. The mentor program costs $490.

The New South Wales Department of State and Regional Development's 'Stepping Up' program is for higher-level proprietors. The 'Women in Business' program has three core programs, which cover planning, sales and finance, and includes a metropolitan six-month program, a regional three-month program and a growth strategy workshop held every year. Visit <www.smallbiz.nsw.gov.au> for more information.

Women Chiefs of Enterprises International (<www.wcei.com.au>) is a non-profit national group for women entrepreneurs, aimed at innovation and networking.

Women's Network Australia is an inspirational networking site for like-minded women in New South Wales, Queensland and Victoria (<www.womensnetwork.com.au>). The network is spearheaded by Lynette Palmen, who was awarded an Order of Australia for her community work.

Business Advisory Services are available through the New South Wales Department of State and Regional Development. For your nearest centre, call 1300 650 058.

Signature recipe:
Bella Serventi's fluffy pink cupcakes

500g butter
750g sugar
10 eggs
500g self-raising flour
1 teaspoon vanilla essence
dash of full-cream milk

Icing
300g butter
300g hot water
red food colouring
icing sugar

Preheat your oven to 180°C. Cream the butter and sugar using a mixer, then slowly mix in the eggs. Fold in the flour gently—don't overwork it, or the cupcakes won't be fluffy! Add the vanilla essence and milk, stir gently again and drop the mix into cupcake moulds. Bake for 25 minutes.

To make the icing, combine the butter and hot water. Add in two to three drops of red food colouring, then whisk in your icing sugar—keep adding it until the icing gets a thick consistency. Spread the icing onto the cooled cupcakes, and serve them with hot chocolate and marshmallows!

Chapter 10
Top Tips from Cluey Cooks

> *If someone is making decisions for you, it's very difficult to learn.*
>
> —Elle Macpherson, speaking with *The Australian Financial Review*

Just finding a good sounding board in life isn't easy, let alone getting help with your financial problems. And unless you're lucky enough to have family support, mentors and role models can be thin on the ground when you really need them — at the beginning of your investing journey or the start of a new business or career.

Fortunately, one thing that savvy gals share is the happy knack for taking control and creating a path — sometimes with support and sometimes without. Whatever their strategies, most women have a clear idea of their financial direction and timing. And while getting professional advice is great, it's not a magic pill or a replacement for understanding your money. Sound like a catch 22? Louise Brogan, All Money Matters founder and former member of the Australian Securities Exchange, explains that bringing in outside help doesn't mean handing over your authority to act, but 'can be really useful as a way of getting ideas, creating some accountability for your actions and having an external perspective on your situation'.

Good advice isn't just about someone asking you the right questions at the right time, either: it's also about being taught something or offered an insight that you couldn't get for yourself. As we mentioned in chapter 5, you need to be 100 per cent clear that you're getting value for your money if you engage an adviser.

✳* Good advice basics

Vivienne James, director of the advice arm of Investec, offers some practical principles:

- *Choose the right adviser.* Find one who's both technically and investing savvy. Consider taking along someone who's also an expert in these areas to verify the adviser's knowledge and experience. If you've got the name of the adviser through a referral, be thorough in your assessment. Being numerate and understanding tax implications is important in an adviser; however, from a portfolio management perspective, being able to look at investment options is what counts.
- *Seek independence.* Impartiality and a lack of bias are critical in an adviser. If you have a large amount of funds to invest, it's usually preferable to opt for a fee-for-service arrangement rather than pay through commissions and trails (the latter being a flat fee embedded in the fund's fees for the adviser's benefit only). Over the

life of an investment, trails can become a considerable cost.
- *Manage risk.* Know what your expectations are. It's no good selecting high-return investments if you're a conservative investor, because you're likely to panic and sell in the down cycle.
- *Asset allocation is key.* Over the long term, it's generally the spread of assets and how much you invest in each that drives your performance—93 per cent of performance, in fact. It can be helpful to remember this when you're agonising over selecting the best-performing stock!
- *Have a strategy.* If you have a detailed plan in place, you'll be more likely to weather the cycles and achieve a better performance.

* First appeared in 'Mo' Money' by Julianne Dowling, *Vive* magazine, February/March 2007, p. 102.

In the last chapter, we got the lowdown from five women on starting and running a business. But how do women with financial know-how deal with their own money? In this final chapter, we'll hear from seven women who are prominent in the finance world on how they walk the talk:

- Ranjana Sengupta and her daughter Rashmi Mehrotra are both pioneers in wealth advice. Ranjana was one of the first advisers in the financial planning industry, while Rashmi heads up the retail services of research house Mercer Investment Consulting. Rashmi's one of a powerful group who help direct financial planners on investment trends and strategies for their clients.

- Anne-Marie Spagnolo is a Melbourne-based financial planner and partner in Ethical Investment Services, and author of *The Ethical Investor: Make Money and Feel Good About It* (Penguin 2007).
- At 24, Amber Werchon runs one of Ray White's top Queensland sales teams, has won state and national sales awards for her work in Queensland real estate, and already has a portfolio of seven properties.
- Katrina Pulbrook is one of ANZ's senior Financial Planners in Melbourne.
- Shelley Fearnley is a risk broker specialising in women's personal and life insurances through her business, Pearl Insurance.
- Jo-Anne Bloch is CEO of the Australian Financial Planning Association.

Measure the ingredients: Ranjana Sengupta and Rashmi Mehrotra*

'Rashmi and I are similar in our (investing) styles', Ranjana says. Neither are interested in owning property directly, although Rashmi is looking at opportunities in India where the yields can be 10 per cent or more. She adds that it's a pity Australian women love their residential property so much, as the rental yields here have languished at around 2 per cent! Maybe this love, she ponders, has turned us into a nation of conservative investors:

* First appeared in 'Mo' Money' by Julianne Dowling, *Vive* magazine, February/March 2007, pp. 102–103, and since updated.

> Security doesn't come from buying a house. My family had such an immense amount of property and that put me off it. You're concentrating on the property and putting so much time and energy into managing it.
>
> I've changed from active investments such as shares to managed investments. I haven't got the time to look at my share portfolio enough, as my business is quite big and clients come first. So my portfolio is about managed funds.

Ranjana urges women to learn to take responsibility for their money, as more than a few women have come to her after a bad brush with an accountant or an adviser. Maybe sign up for courses on shares or become a super fund trustee!

Daughter Rashmi explains that she approaches her personal wealth by dividing it up into three mental accounts: long-term, medium-term and play money:

> By dividing up my wealth into notional accounts, I can assign different time frames and risk profiles to them. Before I even started investing, though, I insured my income and put enough money aside in a cash management trust to last six months without pay.
>
> The long-term super money is invested in shares and diversified alternatives. For my medium-term portfolio, I'm trying to build a diversified portfolio of income streams. The play money is 'aspirational' — I want to invest it in high-return ideas. For example, I could invest in private equity, either my own business or somebody else's.

Given the nature of my job, I end up applying the same rigorous research filters to my personal investments as I do when researching investments for clients. The biggest mistake people make is to ignore valuation — they overpay for the asset.

Prepare with care: Anne-Marie Spagnolo on ethical investing

These days, most people try to minimise their water and energy use and reduce their carbon footprint on the planet. Did you know there's now evidence to support the idea that ethical investing is not only good for us, but profitable as well? The Ethical Investment Association has done a study which compares the average ethical-fund returns to the returns of mainstream funds: over five years, the ethicals outperformed the others by 2 per cent per annum!

Anne-Marie Spagnolo got interested in ethical investing after spending time in Africa, including two years living and working in Mozambique. She felt that companies (and governments) could do more about social justice issues:

> You could really see the suffering and mostly, in the developed world, we are oblivious to it…so it got me thinking. When I got into workforce and looked at super and investing, I wanted to make sure the companies were doing the right thing.

Think carefully about what you want to screen out from your investments — maybe uranium mining, biotechs, some or all resources? If you're going for managed funds, be aware that there are many different ethical investment funds, and their approaches vary. Some, for example, will invest in the most ethical company in each sector, which may include the 'most ethical' tobacco company—some people have issues with that! Take a look at the funds' websites for details of their investment strategies, and contact them directly if your questions aren't answered.

Finding out what's going on in your super fund can be more difficult, Anne-Marie warns:

> You need to lobby the super fund trustee and demand to know what's happening. Most investors don't have a clue what's going into their super fund. You'll also have more power if you can pool with other members—so if you're in an industry fund, lobby and write a petition letter to the trustee. If you can't find out [what the fund is investing in], it's a reason to move.

Australian Ethical Investments disclose which companies they invest in online, she points out—why don't others?

She also laments the fact that many financial planners don't support ethical investment:

> They still think it's a green feral world, but it's not. Or they think that ethical investors are hippies—and they're not. These days, it's a broad base: we get young women needing a super fund who are keen, and we also have retirees. Four years ago, 70 per cent of our clients were women, but that's dropped back now.

It has been a little skewed to the caring professions, teachers, artists and creatives such as architects, but again, that's changing. Now that people are hearing that the returns are better, they're interested, and since ethical companies often have more sustainable returns, people see that as attractive [in itself].

Anne-Marie works out her personal spending, saving and investing amounts by looking at what she needs to live on and save or invest, and putting the rest into super:

> I salary-sacrifice and think everyone should. I have friends on high salaries and they don't do it. People feel that superannuation contributions disappear down a black hole!
>
> My super is in ethically screened funds and my non-super investments are in ethical managed funds and direct shares. I 'stock-pick' individual stocks: I don't differentiate between income- and growth-oriented companies, because I prefer to understand a company and its outlook. The other thing is the share price. Finding a company may be easy, but you still need to do financial analysis.
>
> Personally, I avoid the resources sector completely, because even though mining companies are becoming more environmentally aware, they still have a long way to go in the developing world in my opinion, and need to show more leadership. The other reason is that they are carbon-intensive industries. I prefer renewable-energy companies.
>
> When you look at the environmental footprint, a company that's reducing its carbon footprint makes

cost savings, so it will perform better. A mining company that rehabilitates well is less likely to be exposed to legal actions, their insurance premiums will be lower...it all flows to the bottom line and makes sense.

However, being a financial planner has made me realise that you can't fulfil everyone's objectives using ethical investment screens. To date in Australia, property and fixed-interest asset classes don't offer much in the way of ethically screened product. In fixed interest the money is pooled, so you don't know what it's being used for. I'm hoping that in five years' time we'll see fixed-interest funds that are socially responsible or have a filter on them...I also hope that in 10 years' time we'll see some leadership in property trusts, and they'll focus on six-star energy-rated buildings. Regulations are making that more possible.

For me, sometimes, it's a trade-off between financial objectives and ethical concerns, but I'll always prefer to use ethical investments if I can.

Mix in some property: Amber Werchon

Young professionals are pretty keen on property, partly because it's getting easier for young women to borrow finance, and partly because they tend to have higher paid jobs, so there's a tax incentive. At 24, Amber Werchon is a bit more than just 'keen': she has a staggering seven properties (four residential and three commercial). This phenomenal achievement is the result of sheer hard work and a dogged savings discipline—while Amber's parents went guarantor for her early loans, she took multiple jobs to raise the deposits herself.

Investing in property at an early age can pay huge dividends, as capital gains tend to get better the longer you hold a property. Traditionally, property values tend to run on 5-year to 10-year cycles: you have to be prepared to wait for the cake to cook!

Amber's success may seem unattainable to many women, but her attitude is, 'Where there's a will, there's a way'. Her goal is to buy one property a year: the general plan is 'buy, hold, build up equity, repeat'. It's important, she says, to know your 'equity ratio'—that is, how much equity you have in your properties—so you can borrow more money to invest. You don't necessarily have to be a mega-high-earner to follow Amber's lead, just make sure you can cover any shortfalls in rents and are able to benefit from the tax-deductible expenses.

In Amber's case, she makes a point of being neutrally geared. That means she has only one property whose rent doesn't cover the mortgage, 'so I never lose anything. I still fix the interest rates and prepay interest'. Fixing interest on an investment property is a popular strategy, because you have set repayments over your three or five years and don't need to pay down the principal amount. This is good debt rather than bad, because it's tax-deductible.

Amber's property recipe

- Start saving now! The sooner you get a deposit, the better. The first one is the hardest.

- Speak to a financial adviser to set up a plan for your investment strategy.
- Discuss your financial objectives with your parents to see if they can provide some equity to get you into the market.
- You can purchase most properties with a 5 per cent deposit or a deposit bond, but try to save 10 per cent—it demonstrates your capacity to save and helps you should the market change. Personally, I always put 20 per cent on residential properties to avoid mortgage insurance (a bank requirement).

Add advice and stir: Katrina Pulbrook

Melbourne-based ANZ Financial Planner Katrina Pulbrook has her own self-managed super fund but, as she says, they aren't for everyone:

> Often, self-managed super funds don't make sense unless you have a lot of money to invest; and even then, compliance has become a lot tougher. DIY super funds really only work for people who have the right of amount of knowledge, time and money (the general view is over $250 000, but it depends on individual circumstances). Anything less than $50 000 in super means you should consider a professionally managed super fund that provides diversification. You may also want to explore other options, such a wrap service with direct shares.

Take care if you're going into a fund with other family members; you have to agree on the same investments and navigate around issues that may cause disputes.

Having a self-managed fund and selecting your own investments can be a fad, too: over time, the novelty wears off and it may become a chore. A SMSF can be good for a small-business owner who wants to finance a commercial property for the business in their name and have some ownership in the super fund. It can also be great during a bull market. But people often find the running of a SMSF very tasking.

Whatever type of superannuation fund they choose, however, she stresses that it's vital to prioritise putting money into it:

> The interrupted pattern in women's super starts early, and it really does affect the compounding on their savings. Women have career breaks or take the secondary earning role when they have children.
>
> Some single women put money into super but their first priority is a home. If you're smart, you can have both. But if you start saving into super at age 45, you just won't have the same balances as the person who starts at 25: the gap is too great. Depending upon what stage of life you're at, it can be beneficial to put the minimum amount into your mortgage and the rest into super, because once you hit the preservation age you can access the funds and pay down the debt at that point. Putting larger amounts of money into super obviously makes sense as you age.

As well as her super fund, Katrina has a wide spread of other investments:

> I've got another geared investment portfolio, and I have four residential properties and a half-share in another. I've learned as I get older that I'm paid for my time to do what I do, and I need to pay someone else to save me time. So I've got a great property manager, but yes, I do look after my own investments.
>
> I'm a high-risk person, and that's about self-belief and my own skill set. If you have covered off every area and have a good spread of investments — that's important. In terms of managed funds, I have a mix of investment managers and investment styles, because you don't want just one style. I manage the debt levels, and I'm probably more conservative in that area.
>
> Estate planning is also vital, in order to know that what will happen with the money after you go. An accountant and a family member together can be a good choice for the trustee. In your will, you should also state who you want to look after the kids — and you might want to give them some money to cover that extra responsibility! Estate planning is becoming more intricate with the number of permutations in relationships: better to pay the solicitor to do it properly while you're still alive than for the family to fight it out later.

Katrina sees many divorced women with settlements wondering which way to go financially.

> A key thing when divorcees receive a large amount of money is whether they're emotionally strong enough

to make a long-term decision at that point. It may be best to focus on the short term. Generally, we won't advocate large financial changes until 12 months down the track, although the women are often impatient to move on. I say: slow down and find your way first, because it may change. Sure, you may waste time waiting, but there are lots of ways to make money.

Often, divorcees have the view when they first see a planner that they're coming to 'take the medicine', and they're in denial. But in 12 months' time, they're more open. Sometimes people try to make themselves feel better after a marriage breaks up by spending a large portion of the settlement, so having a budget to spend can be helpful. Don't do any real damage to the money you need to invest. If you have $100 000, then keep $85 000 for investing, not the other way around!

If a divorced woman has a regular income, then they can consider property and other investments. If money is tight, then cash-flow analysis is the first step, to work out what they've got and what they need and where the shortfall is.

Drop in some insurance: Shelley Fearnley

Here's a cautionary tale! Women's risk adviser Shelley Fearnley, of Pearl Insurance, has a female client who fell off a stool, bumped her head and after being extremely dizzy on and off, found she was unable to work for much of the following year. Luckily she had income protection, which covers

75 per cent of your income after an initial wait period, so she was able to weather her disrupted income a little better. Some 60 per cent of women* don't have individual life-insurance protection, and 36 per cent of women have no life-insurance coverage at all!

As well as accidents, Shelley sees claims from women who are suffering from illnesses such as cancer, mental illnesses and chronic fatigue — conditions that knock you out of the workforce for quite a while. In fact, Shelley's mother, a former top real-estate agent, experienced a mystery illness in her middle age that had a huge impact on her finances:

> At 56, she got something similar to chronic fatigue syndrome, although it wasn't ever fully diagnosed. Despite having a lot of tests, she couldn't return to work full-time. The whole thing was unexpected: she was at the top of her game in the real-estate industry. She lived off her savings and worked for friends. It meant a big change in lifestyle, as she found herself on a very tight budget. Eventually she had to sell a block of land that she had intended to build on.

Though her mother had put extra money into super, it wasn't much help in the short term — she didn't retire, because she believed she'd return to work full-time.

Her mother's illness, combined with seeing so many claims go through from people in similar situations, Shelley says, spurred her to take action herself. She's the sole breadwinner for her two girls, so she insured herself thoroughly, taking out

---

* Source: Life Insurance Marketing Research Association, The Garvan Institute of Medical Research 1997.

life insurance, trauma protection and disability insurance and income-protection insurance.

Insurance premiums, Shelley says, depend on your age and your family health history. It's also up to the insurance underwriter to accept your application to become a member, and that can be harder as time goes on and you and your family develop more health problems. A $500000 life-insurance policy may cost less than a $1 a day for a 35-year-old female non-smoker.

> If you have a health issue, then you may get a loading or exclusion or you may be deferred or declined… anything that draws the underwriter's attention will be factored in.

Generally, income-protection policies have a cut-off age of 60, so you need to act beforehand. The older you are, the more expensive the premiums, regardless of how long you've had the policy — unless you have a level-premium policy as opposed to a stepped-premium one. A healthy, non-smoking woman aged 55 working in management and administration will be facing a premium of between $550 and $675 a month for a policy payout of $5000 a month and a wait period of 30 days.

Bear in mind that income protection generally covers only 75 per cent of your income. If you need every dollar of your salary to support your lifestyle, then there's going to be a gap. That's where you should consider supplementary policies. For example, trauma policies have tax-free lump-sum payouts, which can be useful for expensive hospital bills.

However, the premiums for trauma insurance can be more expensive than for other cover, depending upon your history and age—'but it's better to have something in place rather than nothing, because of the high payouts', says Shelley.

Generally, the policies cover serious health events such as heart attack, cancer and stroke...and possibly up to 45 other events as well, including conditions such as motor neurone disease, multiple sclerosis and severe burns.

Studies by the Investment and Financial Services Association show that women tend to regard insurance as too pricey and too hard. But they should consider some—even if it's just for income protection, says Shelley.

> Women aren't acknowledging their own value in the family and protecting themselves. If they weren't there tomorrow, then how much would it cost to replace them?

Shelley's insurance recipe

- Consider how you'd survive if you were unable to work for three months, six months or longer.
- What would the financial impact be on your family if you were to die prematurely?
- Check if you have any insurance with your super fund and whether it's enough.
- If you have a policy, review it to ensure it's still the best and most appropriate cover.
- Check the cover your spouse has. If they were to die prematurely, is there enough cover for you and the family to survive on?

Enjoy the fruits of planning: Jo-Anne Bloch

Jo-Anne Bloch, the CEO of the Financial Planning Association of Australia, had her first brush with a financial planner about 12 years ago after she and her husband realised they'd be vulnerable if they lost their jobs—they had two dependants and were paying off a mortgage.

> We'd never saved enough: we'd put money into super and then blow the rest. Suddenly the prospect emerged that one of us could lose a job and I thought 'Oh my God…what will happen?'

Fortunately, a friend in a financial planning firm recommended her to a woman who, in Jo-Anne's words, 'was strong enough to deal with me and be someone I'd listen to'.

> I knew we needed a budget and had to do something different. But I also knew we had to be involved from the outset. You can't say to someone who likes spending, 'Well, you're on a diet now—stop spending!' There's a lot of emotional behaviour around what women will do with money, and saving isn't always the first thing that they think about. So we learned to pay the mortgage and the super, and a bit extra into a savings account, first. We lived on the balance.

Jo-Anne's message to women thinking about getting paid advice is to remember that it's not a passive decision; you still have to be involved:

> We want literate and engaged consumers—people who question what their advisers are saying! If your

trusted adviser recommends gearing, for example, you need to ask questions, and if you aren't comfortable, ask if there are other ways to achieve the [desired] outcomes.

It's about deciding what to work on together and then establishing the goals. And it's about asking stupid questions when you can't understand the detail—and also about understanding the remuneration. If you're not happy with the amount that's being asked, try and negotiate a discount.

A lot of women manage the family budget. If you can do that, you just need to translate it into the bigger picture. [An adviser can help] raise your confidence level and bridge from what you're familiar with.

Jo-Anne says she herself is an extremely conservative investor—'If I don't understand it, I don't do it'. She and her husband have a small share portfolio with blue-chip shares and other shares that have long-term potential. Her husband is also part of a defined benefits superannuation scheme, and they take up every benefit they can, she says, because the fund features are generous and cost-effective:

> We have managed funds and only one dud international investment—it's paid its way for 12 years, but it should have done better. Now, I've tipped as much as I can into super…I may liquidate some managed investments before June 2007 but we're only talking $15 000. I've had eight super funds, and so I wanted to consolidate them all into a flexible master trust which also has good insurance benefits.

We pay our adviser by commission, which is great, because I can ring them when I want to and I don't have to write a cheque. The fees are all disclosed so we know how much we're paying, and some of it is rebated. And the planning firm is very up-front. When I came back from the UK, the planners did a new strategic plan, which was very helpful.

But again, you can only outsource so much. You have to keep on top of it. One of my strategies is to keep it simple—maybe that's to our detriment, but at least I understand what we're doing and get advice when needed. We don't gear with shares because I believe that when gearing is popular you're probably at the end of the cycle, and you have to either stick with the knitting or have a very long-term horizon to pick up any gains.

Jo-Anne also has a keep-it-simple policy on kids' money:

> My kids have saved money from the day dot, and they're expected to do household chores for no pay—the pocket money is for entertainment purposes. My daughter has a job, and I only supplement her income for travel and emergencies and a few other things. That money goes directly into a bank account.
>
> My advice with kids is start early. Get them to value money, to understand that you need to save to be able to spend. They also need to tone down their lifestyles—they're so consumer-driven! It can cost a fortune covering the kids' frappes, designer jeans, movies and pizzas and the fourth pair of sandshoes!

She's particularly concerned about younger women dialling up big debts on mobile phones:

> If you have a mobile-phone contract, then are you putting yourself into a tough situation? Mobile phones can be a real money trap. It's great to find a phone plan that works for you, but as I asked my daughter, who's going to fund it? We've agreed the prepaid cards don't work so well for teens with higher usage levels though — they're expensive.

The FPA has resource tools for all ages online at <www.fpa.asn.au>, including a money-sense program for young Australians called DollarSmart and information on retirement, finding a financial planner and other issues. It's well worth a look.

Bon Appetit!

So there you have it: all the recipes you need to begin your journey to financial success and freedom! To finish, here's a reminder of the key strategies covered in this book, courtesy of ANZ Financial Planning's Katrina Pulbrook:

- *Take action.* Develop your financial nous well before pre-retirement, or you may feel desperate!
- *Have a financial goal in mind.*
- *Educate yourself.* Maybe you need to find a financial mentor, read some books on money and investing, talk to friends about your money and work out what's holding you back financially.
- *Reduce your spending.* Check over everything that you spend on, including insurances and loans, see what

sort of savings you can make, and put those savings aside or use them to pay off debt. With the help of compounding interest (that's interest on the original amount, plus interest on the interest!), small amounts can add up to something substantial over time.
- *Consider giving up bad debt and non-deductible debt.* Look at reducing any debt that can't be claimed as a tax deduction. Your house is an appreciating asset, but your credit card isn't helping you on any level!
- *Diversify your wealth.* Make sure your money's spread over different investments — property, shares, bonds, and so on — even if your money's all in a super fund.
- *Increase your income.* Get a job, ask for a raise or a bonus, turn a hobby into a business. 'This can make you more valuable and really enhance your self-esteem! You work for yourself, in the end, so don't undervalue your contribution. The money you make is for YOU', says Katrina. Don't be a work potato!

These simple but effective strategies can make a world of difference — it's all about the money, honey!

Kids' hit:
Jo-Anne Bloch's Crunchie ice-cream

2 L good vanilla ice-cream
3 Crunchies, crumbled

Take the ice-cream out of the freezer for a while. When it's soft, mix the Crunchies and ice-cream evenly, ensuring Crunchies are still chunky. Pour into a 2 L cake tin and freeze.

When you're ready to eat, put the cake tin in hot water for 20 seconds and then turn out onto a plate. Decorate with more Crunchies and enjoy!

Index

Adams, Jessica 89–90, 100
advice and tips, summary 207–228
advisers, choosing 160–161, 208–209
allocated pensions 99, 135, 138, 142
anti-detriment payments 93–94
asset allocation 140, 209
Australian Business Number (ABN) 187
Australian Securities Exchange 167
automatic debits as a saving strategy 37–38

bank accounts 178–179
bankruptcy 153
Bloch, Jo-Anne 210, 224–227
brokers
—full-service 168
—online 166
Brooks, Kirsty 42–43, 55–56
budgeting 25–36
—case studies 28–34, 35–36
—creative approach 2–4
—procrastination 26

capital gains tax 79, 90, 134, 152, 188

caring for others 101–125
—ageing parents 105–113
—children 102–105
—dependants with disabilities or chronic illness 114–117
cash flow 34–36
Centrelink pension
—assets test 98–99, 108–110, 137
—drought relief 118–119
child care 102–105
Child Care Benefit 36, 102–103
Child Care Tax Rebate 36–37, 104–105
children and money 226–227
Christmas spending 24–25
compounding 140, 228
Cowling, Jo 11, 19
credit cards 10, 39–54
—case studies 46–52
—credit files 45–46
—effect on ability to take out a loan 62
—management of 41–54

debt 15, 39–54
—case study of bad debt 48–52
—reduction of bad debt 46–54
depreciation and tax 77–78, 80

discretionary spending 21–24
diversification 153,
    159–160, 165, 217
divorce 69–70, 90–92,
    134, 219–220
    —money case study 13
    —property case studies 69–70
    —superannuation case studies
        129, 148–149, 150–152
downsizing 143
drought relief 118–119
Dye, Bianca 64–65, 81

education, investing for 11,
    15, 115, 175–180
education plans 179
entrepreneurs *see* small
    business start-ups
estate planning 219
ethical investing 212–215

family, sharing equity with 67–69
Fearnley, Shelley (Pearl
    Insurance) 220–223
financial advisers *see*
    advisers, choosing
financial personality test 5–8
Financial Planning
    Association 133, 227
First Home Owner
    Grant 62, 63, 66
freelancing 34–36, 42–43, 90
friendly society bonds 179–180

gearing *see* margin loans,
    negative gearing
goals, setting 2–3, 8–14, 26
Gold, Bex (Cinderella) 194–196

identity fraud, prevention of 46
impulse shopping 21–24

insurance 120–123, 220–223
    —bonds 179–180
    —health 31, 34, 120, 223
    —home and contents 122–123
    —income protection 220–223
    —landlord's 34, 70, 74, 123
    —life 93
    —mortgage 62
    —small business 187–188
    —superannuation funds and 130
    —trauma 222–223
investing
    —choosing an adviser 160–161
    —diversification 159–160
    —managed funds 161–164
    —passive 163–164
    —products 158–159
    —properties 70–80
    —risks 158–159
    —timing 159

Jaye, Kylie 157–158

managed funds 161–164, 177
margin loans 172–175
McGregor, Ali 35–36, 38
McKevitt, Anne 190–191
Mehrotra, Rashmi (Mercer
    Investment Consulting)
    209, 210–212
mentors 184, 203–204
money management *see* budgeting
mortgages 60–63
    —advice for the over-fifties 97
    —insurance 62
    —low doc loans 61–62
    —offset accounts 178
    —paying off faster 67
    —rate comparisons 61
    —shared equity 63
    see also reverse mortgages

negative gearing 70, 75–79
net worth 14–18
—case study 16–18
—definition 14
—tips 14–16

overspending 21–25

pension *see* allocated pensions, Centrelink pension
Posener, Carol (Get Organised) 198–203
property 57–80
—case studies 64–67, 68–72, 74–75, 215–217
—deductions 79–80
—depreciation 78, 80
—distribution following relationship breakdown 69
—insurance 73–74
—investing in 70–80
—management of 72–74
—negative gearing 75–79
—renovation 63–64
—selection criteria 59–60
—sharing equity in 67–69
see also mortgages
Pulbrook, Katrina (ANZ) 210, 217–220

real estate *see* property
recipes
—Ali McGregor's braciola 38
—Bella Serventi's fluffy pink cupcakes 205
—Bianca Dye's tuna salad 81
—Jane Rutter's brilliant fruit tart 156
—Jane Toohey's classic spag bol 181

—Jessica Adams' gourmet seafood pizza 100
—Jo-Anne Bloch's Crunchie ice-cream 229
—Jo Cowling's Thai chicken & lychee salad 19
—Kirsty and Mark Brooks' vegieburgers 55–56
—Monica Trapaga's pasta salad 126
reframing 3–4
renovating property 63–64
retirement 12, 95–99, 109–112, 132–133, 135, 137–138, 140–144, 153–154, 159, 173
reverse mortgages 110–113, 143, 144
risk 4–8, 158–160
rural women 117–120
Rutter, Jane 154–155, 156

sandwich generation 103–104, 123–125
saving *see* budgeting, goals
self-managed superannuation funds (SMSFs) 139, 150–152, 217–218
Sengupta, Ranjana 209, 210–212
Senior Australians Equity Release Association of Lenders (SEQUAL) 111, 112
Serventi, Bella 191–194, 205
share clubs 168–170
shares 165–172, 178
—case studies 168–171
singles 83–99
small business start-ups 183–204
—case studies 185–188, 190–203
—financial tips 185–189

—insurance 187–188
—mentors 184, 203–204
—plans 186, 200
—superannuation 152–154
Spagnolo, Anne-Marie (Ethical Investment Services) 210, 212–215
spending
—addiction to 21–24
—celebrity-style 39
—data on women's and men's habits 40
—generation Y 40
—tips for avoiding 23–24
superannuation 127–155
—access to 142, 146–148, 154
—age-related restrictions on contributions 136
—asset allocation 140–141
—bankruptcy 153
—calculating how much you will need 141–142
—changing funds 139–140
—consolidating accounts 141
—divorce settlements 134
—finding lost super 86
—life insurance 93, 130
—limits on undeducted contributions 136, 147–148, 152–153
—overseas pension funds 146–148
—payments to spouse and dependants 94–95
—pension versus lump sum 142–143
—reasonable benefit limits, abolition of 135–136, 145–146
—recent changes to 34–137
—self-employment 136
—simplified superannuation 133–134
—small business owners 152–154
—social security changes 137
—sources of advice 86, 133, 141
—super splitting 145–146
superannuation co-contributions 131, 134
superannuation funds, self-managed 139, 150–152

tax
—Child Care Tax Rebate 36–37
—expatriate income and assets 89
—investments 172–180
—offsets 36
—property 69–70, 75–80
—superannuation 134–136
—work-related expenses 36
Trapaga, Monica 123–125, 126

Veda Advantage 40, 45

Ward, Meredith (Autism Victoria) 114–117
Werchon, Amber (Ray White) 210, 215–217
widows 92–95
wish list *see* goals, setting
women
—in their fifties 9, 12–14, 95–99
—in their forties 9, 12–14, 90–92
—in their thirties 9, 10–12, 86–90
—in their twenties 8–10, 84–86